Class Lessons with Joel Goldsmith

This collection of tape transcripts represent the most pure form of
Joel Goldsmith's teaching of the message of the Infinite Way. Most
of Joel's writings were constructed from the transcripts which
comprise his audio recordings.

© Copyright 2008 – BN Publishing

www.bnpublishing.com

info@bnpublishing.com

Contents

1. The True and False Sense of "I"

Have you ever had a problem that did not involve the word "I"? Try to think — think now. Have you ever had problem that did not concern the word "I", or that wouldn't have been eliminated if there hadn't have been an I?

When a person commits suicide do they do away with the problem or the I that had the problem, in their own belief? They can't do away with the problem, can they? They do away with the I or at least they believe that. And that's the attempt — that's what they're doing when they attempt suicide — "I have a problem and if I'm out of the way that ends the problem." There's more truth to fiction in that. If I am out of the way, I can have no problem. And the only problem that anyone ever has is I. I — I am the only one that ever has my problem. And if there were just no I, I would have no problem. So the troublemaker is I. Oh, if I just do away with I, what a nice sweet life I would have — not a single problem. Now today that's what we hope to accomplish. Today we want to fulfill that part of the Bible's teaching that says, "I die daily." Only let's hurry up the process. Instead of dying by bits and having it so rawn out and painful let's do it all in one job today, and see if we can't die one beautiful rand death, so that we may be reborn of the Spirit.

There is only one reason for discords or disharmonies of any nature. And that reason is a false sense of I. The correct sense of I would eliminate every problem from the face of the Earth — personal, family, community, national, and international. There's only one error on this entire Earth, and the error is a false interpretation or a false sense of I. As long as I think that I for instance must make a living or find a home or decide what to do next year, just that long will I be facing problems of one nature or another. If I ever come to a place of realization of the grand truth that has been revealed in the Bible (it was revealed originally about 4,000 years B.C.E.). I don't even know about originally, but at least we have knowledge that the teaching of Krishna about 4,000 B.C.E. is all on the subject of "I", and of course, all of Shankara's Advaita teaching of India is entirely on the word "I".

Now these great revelations reveal that the only I is God. And that God as individual being is living its life as you and as me. The Word became flesh and dwelt among us. The word God became individualized as you and as me, and dwells here as us. But, we have entertained through the years a false sense of that I, and instead of recognizing that the I is God, we have taken the I to ourselves as person, built up an identity and then tried to maintain it and sustain it. We might say that it would be something like a millionaire forgetting that he was a millionaire and then starting to worry about how to make a living and how to pay his rent. And then somebody saying to him, "But you are a millionaire." And he says "Oh, yes, in reality I am, but of course, in belief I still [am poor]." Yes, but why have the belief if in reality you are a millionaire? Why not give up the belief? Well, so in our Truth teaching we all admit that in reality, "I am the image of God, the son of God." Well, then why have problems? "Oh, because in belief I am a mortal." Well, then why not give up the belief? Let the other fella believe it, and why not let us give up the belief since it's only because of belief that we are struggling with mortality.

Now this is very clearly illustrated in an incident in scripture. Judas Iscariot has committed suicide. There are only eleven disciples left, and they have met together for the purpose of selecting a twelfth to replace Judas. And as they meet a prayer is voiced. And the prayer is this, "Father, show us whom Thou hast chosen." Now there you have the whole sense of what I'm trying to bring out. Not one of those eleven thought that I am responsible for voting for the right fellow or selecting the right disciple. Not one fellow used the word "I". Not one of them thought that it was any of their business who was elected or selected. They all were in agreement, "Father show us whom Thou hast chosen."

Well, supposing we have a decision to make today. And I say to myself, "I must make that decision sometime today. I have only 'til noon to make that decision." And when I sit down and I might even turn to God and say, "God, what decision should I make?" or "Show me what decision to make." And you know, I am apt not to make a decision or apt not to make the right one — the word "I" is in there. Whereas why should I not accept the fact that since God governs and directs my experience, why shouldn't I say, "Father show me what decision you have made today, since this is your life, it's your universe, it's your world, how would you like it run in this connection? What decision would you like to have made manifest? Show me your decision." And, then of course, not only you'll show me your decision but you'll even carry it out. Whereas if I look for a decision I will then try to carry it out, won't I? Two blunders instead of one. First I'm making a decision and then I'm concerning myself with carrying out my decision and all this time I had no right to make the decision or to carry it out. So the word "I" got me into one blunder. The same word "I" got me into the second blunder.

Well now, in some of my writings you will find chapters on that, or at least one chapter in one of the classes, I think it's "Matthew Speaks," on the very subject of I as the devil. Well, that I is a devil that would try to make a decision isn't it? That I that concerns itself with how this universe should be run, how God's business should be run, that I is a devil. As a matter of fact to be completely correct, that I that I am entertaining isn't an I at all, it's a false sense of I. The real sense of I is God. Any other sense of I is an error. Therefore, there is not really a God and a devil. There's not really a power of good and a power of evil. There's no such thing as a power of evil. There is only the infinite power of good. But then there is that false sense of that power which we entertain called personal sense. Personal sense is really the only devil. And we eliminate all error the minute we eliminate the personal sense of I.

2. The God of Our Lives

Remember this — that the greatest blessing that has come to the human world has been the denial of the Master by those He fed and healed, and the denial of the Master by his very disciples. Because in that experience we have learned not to trust man whose breath is in his nostrils, not to place our faith in the outer world, but always to turn within and become acquainted with our guardian angel, with our angel of the Lord, with our divine protector, with the very image of God which has been planted in the midst of us since the beginning of all time.

Men fashion their kingdoms of temporal power, of gold, silver, brass, and clay. We read of these temporal kingdoms in the seventh chapter of Daniel. We learn here of the finite temporary nature of the kingdoms of this world. The 34th verse of this chapter of Daniel we read that a new kingdom shall be set up which will never be destroyed. This kingdom is carved out of a stone that is cut out of a mountain without hands. This stone destroys all temporal kingdoms and the work of men. Think of this — a stone carved out of a mountain without hands. Is not this the work of God? And the kingdom that shall stand forever, is not that the reign and realm of the Messiah? The power that rules not by might nor by power but by my spirit. The human life constituted of gold and silver and brass and iron, mixed with clay, is a kingdom divided against itself. And spiritual wisdom alone, the still small voice, can destroy it and reveal the kingdom of immortality under the government of love.

As faith and confidence in men and metals and minerals is displaced, and the understanding of God as substance replaces material sense, the power and glory of the new consciousness appears. My kingdom is not of this world. The ministering angels within our own consciousness, the impartation of the spiritual word within — this makes for us the safety, security, harmony, joy, and peace of our world.

3. The Realized God

I have been asking our students and will continue to ask, that they give one period of their meditation each day to God alone. Not for themselves, not their family, not for their business, not for their patients or students, and not even for peace on Earth, but for God alone. In other words reserve one period for a meditation in which we come to God with clean hands.

Father I seek nothing. I'm not seeking anything for anybody. I am not come here to accomplish anything or to achieve anything. I'm coming here in the same spirit that I would go to my mother were my mother available. Just for a visit. Just for a communion. Just for love. The love between me and my mother is of such a nature that I would love to sit by her, or walk by her, or sit at her feet, or take a ride. I would love to be in her company, oh, I don't mind if it's days, weeks, months, or if occasionally I could have just 2 or 3 minutes of her time alone. I want nothing of my mother. I seek nothing. Just the joy of being in her company and feeling that joy that naturally flows from a mother to a son, to a child. That's why I'm here today. You are the Father and Mother of my being. You are the Source of my life. You are the Soul of me, the Spirit of me. You are that which makes me tick. And I come in this period just for the joy of communion. I have no favors to ask. No desires. Just let us pass this moment together, in communion. So that where Thou art, I am. And that I remember where I am, Thou art for we be One. Just for the joyous awareness that I am in Thee, and thou art in me. Yes, if it can be, just to feel the assurance of your hand in mine, or the touch of your finger on my shoulder. Thy presence, that's all. Thy presence.

4. Understanding the Body

It seems strange to me at times, although I make very little comment about it, that so little actual study is given to the book "The Infinite Way". It is read and it makes its impression, and the students go back to it occasionally and read some more, but I doubt that there are many that realize that practically every paragraph in this entire book is a metaphysical and spiritual text upon which a whole book could be written — that this book as small as it is, contains everything that we know up to date on the subject of spiritual unfoldment, spiritual living, and spiritual healing. Not a word can be added to this book, or perhaps I should say not a word has ever been added to this book. There isn't a single word in all the writings that isn't originally in this one book. The only thing is that sometimes it is in this book in one sentence and then appears later as a 10,000 or 25,000 word book. But it's the same sentence. It's the same statement. It's the same truth which could have been found in its pure essence and each one work out for themselves instead of having to read another book about it.

Now you will remember as I call it to your attention that the Infinite Way writings declare that the secret of life lies in right identification — that is in knowing our true identity. In knowing who I am or what I am. All of the error in the world — all of the sin, disease, death, lack, and limitation in the world is based only on one ignorance, and that is ignorance of our identity — not knowing who I am or what I am.

Now, of course, in this book "The Infinite Way" the subject is treated quickly, briefly, and with just a statement here and there because it becomes necessary for an individual, for a student, to follow that through to its ultimate conclusion, not for somebody to put it into words for them, because then they'd be living on words instead of inner individual unfoldment.

Also, as this book came through, it came through in such a manner so as not to shock the world into just disregarding it, and so you must naturally expect that ideas are softened here which when you examine them you say, "Do you really mean that that's what it means?" And I do. I mean exactly that.

Now here is a chapter Metaphysical Healing. "Healings are always in proportion to our understanding of the truth about God, man, idea, body." Well, of course, there is just one sentence but as far as I'm concerned I don't know how you could spend less than a year on that one sentence. I don't know how you could possibly not write that sentence out — put it up on the mirror — carry a copy in the purse. And then, regardless of what you are reading for the next year see what it has to say about God, man, idea, body.

You see if we knew the truth about God and man, the truth about idea and body would quickly reveal themselves, because no one who hears these words will ever find their freedom until they know that they are not man. As long as the belief exists consciously or unconsciously or subconsciously within you that you are man, you will be seeking a God — and there isn't any to be found.

The search for the Holy Grail has been a search for God. Always it has been fruitless. Always it has been a failure until the individual came home broke in health, broke in mind, broke in body, broke in purse, and there discovered it hanging right up on there on tree, or buried within their own garden, in other words, within their own being.

Now, in the chapter Supply in this book I gave the secret, but evidently too few of our students have connected up that secret with the whole of being. In the illustration of the orange tree I showed that the oranges do not constitute supply. I don't care how many oranges there are, I don't care how few oranges there are, that has nothing to do with supply. An orange, or any other fruit on a tree, is the product of a life force at work. So the supply is the life force, and the orange is but the fruitage or result or product of the supply. You could have a year without oranges but that wouldn't mean that you were without supply. You could give away your oranges — you could throw them away, and you wouldn't be without supply, because the life force is at work instantly reproducing. So that at most you would have a temporary absence of the result of supply, or product of supply, or fruit of supply.

Now coming back to our identity. Who am I? What am I? And you will find that you are not that which can be supplied. You are supply. You are the law of life operating. I am the life. I am life eternal. I am the life, the way, the truth. I am the bread, the wine, the meat.

Do you not see that everyone including our own students have been trying to demonstrate meat, wine, water, house, health when I am these. I am the life of my body. I cannot get life. I cannot get health. I cannot get supply. I cannot get youth. I cannot get vitality. I am the way, the truth, the life.

Now, as man we would have something to get and we would have something to get it from. We would be eternally seeking a God somewhere to get something for us to give something, but all the way back to Moses it was realized "I am that very I am. I am it." And because of Moses' realization of "I am" or Moses realization that "I am" he was enabled to bring forth a cloud by day, pillar of fire by night, manna from the sky, water from the rock, safety and security for his people all by the realization — what set Moses apart from his people? They were seeking something from "I am" and he was knowing that "I am that I am."

What set him apart from his multitudes? They were seeking to be fed, and he knew he could feed them. They were seeking to be healed, but he knew that he could help them.

Well, there's one tiny sentence in this book that says, "You must know that you are cause and not effect." I don't see how anyone could spend less than three years on that one sentence. I don't know how they possibly can because there isn't a single discord within range of your thought that isn't based on the belief that you are an effect and that there is a cause somewhere that can do something about it.

The mystery of life is in the words "I am."

Now, there is only one answer to the question, "What is God?" And that answer is, "I am." Why is this true? Because if you say, "God is life" you are still leaving yourself out of the picture. "God — is — life." And here am I back here looking up and declaring something out here.

Oh, but you say, "God is love" "God — is — love." Where am I? Left out of that picture because up here is God and over here is love, and here am I looking up there like Oliver Twist asking for a little more.

Well, I am going to leave it with you to ponder this idea of your Self — capital S-e-l-f, as being God Being — Life, Truth, Love, and go from there to the next step which is man. Now remember you are not man. You are life eternal. You are consciousness. You are a state of consciousness. What state of consciousness?

Well, close your eyes for a moment, and now notice that if you are to know anything at all you must know it through your consciousness and that there is not a you and consciousness — that that which is a state of awareness is you. Now, if you are aware of yourself as finite personality that is your state of your consciousness. If you are aware of yourself as infinity, that is your state of consciousness. All right, how can you go from the belief of being a finite being to that of being an infinite being? Again you close your eyes and you ask yourself this, "If I want the answer to something that is back in memory where do I get it?" I go within my own being — I go down deep — and memory gives back to me that which I want to know. Ah, supposing I require today some knowledge — the knowledge of driving an automobile or driving an airplane, or the knowledge of sewing or cooking — where do I go? I go down deep into myself and I draw forth that knowledge. But now supposing I want a knowledge of something heretofore unknown. Let us say there are no automobiles on the road, no airplanes in the sky, no radios, no television. But we've decided there should be these things and there can be these things — now what do we do? We go way, way back into our consciousness and gradually something begins to unfold to put us on the track of some knowledge, and we find more and more and more until ultimately comes forth the entire wisdom that appears as an automobile. Do you remember in

12

this little book ["The Infinite Way"] is the illustration of Marconi? Always these great scientists were spending lifetimes wanting wireless telegraphy but not going toward the invention of it because they first must find what will enable the message to break down the resistance in the air and get through, and Marconi comes along and he knows that there is no resistance. Where did he discover there was no resistance? There wasn't such knowledge in books. Where did he discover that? Where did Moses discover that "I am"? Deep down within themselves. You say, "But there was no such knowledge." No, but you must acknowledge that it existed in infinity — it existed in what we call the mind of God — the soul of God. Well, dig down then into the mind of God. How do you get there? Go into your own mind because that's the only mind there is, and that is God. And you there will find all of the knowledge that is in this world and all of the knowledge that has not yet evolved in this world. There are secrets to be learned about the sun, moon, and stars, and planets that man has never encompassed. But when that knowledge comes forth where do you think it's going to come forth from? From the consciousness of an individual. He's going to find it deep down within himself and bring it forth and write it in a book for us to read. Don't you know that? Don't you know that all knowledge has been found within the consciousness of an individual — then the consciousness of an individual is infinity — and we call that — God.

Truth is within ourselves, according to Browning. "We must open out a way for the imprisoned splendour to escape." But truth is infinite — within ourselves must be infinite. Now can you imagine infinite being sitting around trying to demonstrate supply, health, companionship, and home — when Self is the source of these. So the secret of life then is right identification. Are you life or are you an effect of life? Are you the little oranges on the tree or are you the life force that produces oranges on your tree. That right identification changes your life the very minute that you begin to embody it. The moment that you begin to accept, "Why I am life eternal!" I don't have to go out and get knowledge in a book — that won't make me life eternal. I don't have to go to man whose breath is in his nostril to learn something that will give me more life, youth, or vitality. No, if I must go I must go only for one purpose and that is to learn that I already am that which I am seeking. That which I am seeking, I am. All that God is, I am. Why? The "I" and the Father are one, and "I am" is that one. And when you say, "I am" you are declaring that. Now, that doesn't make your humanness God. That makes your humanness die so that only God is left.

5. The Secret of the Healing Principle

If a righteous person were all the things that scripture credits him with being, and if that could not be imparted to the man in the street—to average you and me—his life would only be that of a miracle worker. And then we could naturally say, "Well, what of it?" Much in the same way that we would go to the theater to watch a great magician. But since we couldn't do those tricks of magic we would just watch this great one perform his things for us.

If the great truths revealed to the spiritual seers of all ages, couldn't be conveyed to the world at large, then these seers would only be so far as we are concerned magicians or miracle workers with no import in our experience. But you see the fact that there has been a dozen of these saints, or more, must indicate that in some way it is possible for us to become aware of these truths, these principles and embody them in our experience. And, if it is possible for us to embody these great truths and demonstrate them and in some measure live them, it must be possible for all mankind. There is no such thing as a law of God which is meant for one man or for one group of men. There is no such thing as a law of God which is meant for us but not for our neighbors outside. It certainly would not be loving our neighbor as ourselves if we believed that we had some capacity for good living that they haven't got.

The secret is this. There is a universal force, a universal belief, a universal hypnotism which is the source of every discord that comes into our experience. Every limitation, every sin, every temptation, every disease that comes to us is but an effect of a universal force or power which remember in and of itself is not power it is only power because of acceptance in the human mind.

If it were a power we couldn't overcome it. If it were a power we couldn't dispel it. It is not a power but to world sense it is the only power which we have to consider in the meeting of sin, disease, death, lack or limitation. In other words what I am trying to say is this, "No person is ever dying." Now try to understand this — no person is ever dying. And if you're ever called upon to help a case of a person who seems to be near death don't try to save their life because you won't succeed. But handle the age old universal belief of a life apart from God — a life which had a beginning and must have ending. Handle the universal mesmerism of death. Because you see there is a universal hypnotism which says that everybody who's born must die. And that same hypnotism says we were born — that we were created of matter — born of man and woman.

Now, this is not a personal belief. This isn't just a belief of you individually as a mother or as a father. This is a universal belief that existed since time began. It is a universal belief in birth which results in a universal belief in death and what we are handling here is not birth or death but the universal belief, the universal hypnotism, which appears as an individual person dying.

Let's put it this way. Close your eyes for a moment. And, let us ... well, let us go over on Sunday afternoon to hear the band — The Royal Hawaiian Band. We're standing in front of the bandstand. And there is a band up on that stand, and everyone up there has an instrument in their hand. The conductor has a baton. And now, is there a single person there? No. Is there a single instrument there? No. But you're sitting, looking directly at it. Yes. But they're not there. No. What is there? What is the fabric of every person you are seeing up on that bandstand? Your imagination is the fabric. Your imagination is the substance out of which those men and those instruments are formed. In fact your imagination is the fabric — the substance of which the whole bandstand is made. So whether, whether now you have human men and women on that platform, metal instruments, or a wooden bandstand, the substance is all the same — imagination. There is no wood there, there is no flesh and blood there, there's no metal there, there is only imagination. Do you follow that? Can you follow that? Do you see that? Do you see that there's no flesh and blood up there? Do you see that there's no wood and no metal up there? That there's only your imagination formed as men, women, wood, metal.

Supposing you were dreaming right now. And now you're dreaming that you're out here in the water. And as you look around you find out that you got out too far and now you can't get back. And now begins your struggle to get back, and there you are out in this water struggling. Is there a you? Is there water? Is there a struggle?

No. What is the fabric or substance of the person you are seeing in the water? What is the fabric and substance of the water? What is the fabric and substance of the struggle? Your dream. Your dream. The dream is the substance, and you and the water and the struggle are the objects — which are formed by your dream.

Now, if we were to take this leather cover and make a man here, and a piano here, and a sky over here, we would still have neither man, piano, nor sky, we would have leather. In the destruction of leather there would be the destruction of the man, the piano, and the sky. In the destruction of your dream there was the destruction of the you in the water, the water, and the struggle. In the destruction of your imagination there was the disappearance of the band and of the instruments and of the bandstand, right? Now, supposing in that first case you'd have started out to eliminate each one of the men from the bandstand. You'd have still been left with instruments after a hard struggle getting rid of all those men. Then you'd have to get to work tearing out those instruments. And after you got through with that you'd have to tear out the bandstand. And you could have done all of that by stopping your imagination in one stroke. Right?

Supposing you were dreaming of struggling in the water. And instead of crying out for someone to rescue you, you just had somebody wake you out of the dream. By the breaking up of the dream, there would be the breaking up of the you in the water, and the water, and the struggle. Right? And so it is.

The fabric of the discords of human experience is a universal hypnotism, a universal belief, or a series of universal beliefs. That's the fabric of every sense of limitation that can come into your experience. Whether it's limited finances, or limited health, or limited family relations, or limited human relations, or limited business, or discordant experiences. The fabric of it is this universal hypnotism — this universal belief of a universe apart from God. Now when a man says, "I have overcome the world." He does not mean that he has overcome all the people in the world, and all the evils of the peoples in the world because his ministry did not last long enough to battle all those people. He overcame the world in one stroke by realizing that the world that needed to be overcome was made up of this mesmeric illusion. And all he had to do was destroy the mesmeric illusion and all the people and all the circumstances and all the conditions of limitation disappeared.

6. How to Pray

Let us pray for anything we want that is not of this world. And I think that you will find that as you take that attitude you will be nearing that of the scripture that says, "We know not what we should pray for." We must let the Spirit bear witness with our Spirit. "We know not what things we should pray for." And it is true, if your prayer is to be limited to that which is not of this world, then you don't know what to pray for, and so your prayer would surely be listening for that Word that proceedeth out of the mouth of God. It wouldn't be any different, than the writers, the painters, the artists, the music composers are up against every day of their lives. They want to bring forth something, but it must be something that had no existence before. There's no use writing a book that's been written before. There's no use painting a picture that's been done before. There's no use inventing an invention that's been invented before. And so how would these men pray?

They would have to learn to turn within for a revelation of something heretofore unknown. And that is an indication of us in prayer. What is the use of our praying for the same things that we've been having for the last 20, 30, 40, 50 years, which have not given us the satisfaction or completeness or perfection after we've gotten them? Of what avail would it be to have a little more of that which hasn't satisfied to begin with? Probably it would be a little more of dissatisfaction come with it. Now, we know not what to pray for. We do know that that which we are seeking is already within us. The whole kingdom of God is within us. The whole of the spiritual universe is within us. We know that. And we know that making statements about it, and reading books about it does not bring it forth. It only leads us to a point where in the silence, or where we are prepared to be in the silence to receive the Grace of God. Here is the secret. We really know what we are seeking. We don't know what things we are seeking. We don't know what things to pray for, but we know what we are seeking. We are seeking the Grace of God, since thy Grace is my sufficiency. We know that.

We know to begin with that we are seeking the Grace of God and nothing but the Grace of God, and we know that we're not going to get it out of the human mind. And we know that we're not going to get it out of a bank account. And we know that we're not going to get it out of the peace that this world can give. And so, since what we are seeking is a Word that proceedeth out of the mouth of God or divine Grace, and since we know that it can only be attained by a state of inner silence, a state of inner awareness — receptivity — it will become necessary for us to prepare ourselves for the experience of receiving that Grace.

The preparation for receiving the Inner Grace are those periods of silence, inner reflection or introspection, meditation or communion.

And even though in those three or four minute periods during the day we seem to be getting nowhere, we seem to be receiving nothing, we seem to be making no progress, don't give up on that account because you have no way of judging any more than you can judge if you decided to take piano lessons and were told to do a five finger exercise, and then at the end of six hours of practice you said, "Well, you know I can't do it any better now than I did at the beginning." Probably that's true. Outwardly it would seem so, but in the first exercise in the scale something started to take place in both mind and muscle. And it might take a whole year of this before what was inwardly taking place could manifest itself in the ability to do that — run right through that scale. But you see it would take each one of those repetitions of that five finger scale even where outwardly there would seem to be no progress, until one arrived at that place where there was a small progress, and so it is with meditation. From the first time that you close your eyes and realize that, "I am seeking the Grace of God. I am seeking some Word that proceedeth out of the mouth of God. I know not what to pray for and so I'm not going to pray for anything of this world." And you see a minute's already gone by but that minute has already emptied us of our human thought about prayer and so for the next half minute at least we have nothing to say. And that's all!

That's all there is to that period of meditation. That alone repeated a dozen times a day would change one's entire life inside of a month. Or, at least it would begin to show changes inside of a month because every time one turned inwardly that way they would be declaring "I can of mine own self can do nothing", even if they didn't think the statement. They would be declaring, "I'm seeking the kingdom within", even if they never thought of those words. Their whole attitude would be "Father I of mine own self can do nothing, come to my rescue." In other words, it would be humility. It would be acknowledging the nothingness of human wisdom, human strength, human power. It would be acknowledging that there must come something from the Infinite Invisible.

Something must come forth from the depths within if we are to be saved. And all of that is the true sense of humility, and it is the true sense of prayer.

In this form of prayer I do not go to God to have certain things brought about for tomorrow or for Holidays.

I don't do that. I go to God in this way:

"Today, tomorrow, and all time to come, God, belong to Thee. Map out my days."

And then I sit in complete silence — in complete quietness as if I really and truly had a telephone receiver at my ear and was trying to hear somebody at the other end. It isn't so much that I expect to hear a voice although I sometimes do. It isn't that I expect that. I'm merely taking that attitude as a symbol of receptivity — just the same as you are sitting here, and if you'll notice this minute you probably have one ear cocked, like this, listening for every word. Now actually you're not too interested whether you hear what I say or not and it isn't too important whether or not you hear what I say. There's no importance in that. The importance is that you sit there with that ear cocked listening because you're not here to hear me at all. That isn't what you came for. You came here to receive the word of God. And it may be that you won't get it from me and that it may not even come through me. But that's not going to be your hard luck. If I don't say a word of truth here tonight it will not effect your demonstration because you haven't come here for me.

You haven't come here for my pleasure or my profit. You've come here because of your own interest in truth. And you've come here to hear truth and you're going to hear it. And if it doesn't come through me it's going to come from God direct to you within you.

You may be sitting there just straining to hear what I'm saying and actually you may not hear it at all, you may be hearing something entirely different than what I'm saying. You may be hearing God speak right within your own being, because every bit of attention that you're giving to me, you are not giving to me at all. I'm as of little interest to you as any other name or face on the face of the globe. What you're here for is your interest in God, your interest in truth and that can't be withheld from you. That's what you came here for. That's what you gave up your time for. That's what you gave up your money and expense for, was to get a message of God and your receptivity is going to bring it to you, and if it doesn't come through my lips it's going to come direct within your own consciousness, or on the other hand if it does come through my lips it won't miss you, you will get it.

Now in the same way — the same attitude that you have in coming here and listening — that same degree of silence and quietness that we have in this room all evening — that is the same attitude of peace and quietness when you're alone in what we will call prayer. Because I want you to know this — that what you are doing here and have been doing ever since I have spoken — you have been praying in my concept of prayer. You haven't been saying a thing to me or to God but you have been listening for the word of truth. And that's prayer. You have been listening for the still small voice and that is prayer. You have been holding yourself receptive to truth, and truth is a synonym for God, therefore you have been holding yourself receptive to God. And that is prayer.

Now this is the highest form of prayer that you can possibly indulge is communion with God, listening for the still small voice, opening consciousness to truth. There's no higher form of prayer than that. That is communion. The mere fact that I am standing here talking doesn't alter the case at all that what you are doing is praying. And if you get an answer to your prayer through what I'm saying it isn't because of me, it's because you've opened your ears to God and God is using my voice with which to answer. But on the other hand if there should be a little obstinacy in me or a little ego in me and God can't break through me to reach you it doesn't mean your time is going to be wasted. You have come here for a message of truth. You have turned your consciousness to God and you will not go out of here without it.

Now you can sit down in your own room and attain the same degree of receptivity you have here, only instead of expecting a voice to come back at you as you're getting from here you will expect merely that God will answer in one way or another. It may be through a voice, it may be through a feeling, it may be through an emotion, it may be through a vision, or and this happens many many times — you may get it without knowing that you've gotten it. In other words, you may get up and say, "Well, nothing happened." But don't be too sure of it. You never know what happens when you open yourself in receptivity to God. You don't always know at that moment but you will know it by the effect in your life. You'll know it by some healing, some increase of supply, some increase of harmony, opportunity. Some form of good will be made manifest in your experience and then you'll remember that that was an answer to prayer that you had been hoping or praying for some such good or thinking about it or knowing that it was right. And now it's here. Now it wasn't your desiring that brought it and it wasn't your wish that you could have it that brought it, it was your prayer. And your prayer was merely opening your consciousness for the word of God.

Remember that the word of God is quick and sharp and powerful. Do you remember that in scripture? And do you remember also that your thoughts are not my thoughts. And my thoughts are not your thoughts saith the Lord. There aren't any of your thoughts that have anything to do with God. It's God's thoughts that determine. And so we are not interested when we go to God in what you or I think. We're not interested even in what we believe or what we hope or what we wish or what we desire, and I don't think God's very much interested either. Because probably we'd get more of the things that we hoped for even though sometimes we'd be sorry for it afterward.

Let us realize this — true prayer is always answered. If you pray and you're prayer is not answered it's because you've prayed amiss. It hasn't been prayer at all no matter what you may have thought it to be. Because true prayer is answered. Now true prayer is the ability to receive the presence and power of God. That's true prayer. When you can at will open yourself to the presence and power of God and let it take over, then you are praying aright.

That form of prayer brings you ultimately to a place referred to by Paul in these words, "I live yet not I, [God] liveth in me." When you come to a place of prayer which is a state of receptivity in which you have no desires, no wants, no hopes, except that God really fulfill Itself in your experience. Remember, "I am come that

20

you might be fulfilled." Once you let that "I" get in, that God, that presence of God, that divine consciousness — It takes over and It fulfills your life.

7. Seek Knock Ask

There will always be hospitals and cemeteries as long as there is somebody unwilling to look the situation right in the face and know that every one of these appearances has existence only as a universal mental belief — a suggestion of a selfhood apart from God, of a law apart from God, as a condition apart from God — as long as there are people willing to believe that God is some great power that can heal disease or enrich them there will be no end to these things called hospitals and cemeteries. They will only come when we individually say, "What is the nature of that which is appearing to us as sin, disease, and death? It's been fooling us long enough, generations enough. What is the nature of this?" and then find out that it's a telephone call about a rumor of something. Why? How did we accept the rumor? Because we didn't know God as the identity of every individual on the face of the globe.

Once we knew that we could reject every rumor and say, "So what? What harm can you do to God?" But what of it? What of it? Is it a power? Is it a presence? No!

So it is with us. What difference does it make? Is there an activity apart from God? Is there a soul apart from God? Is there a being apart from God? Is there a mind? Is there a law apart from God? No — "I know not any," says Isaiah, "I know not any." There are no other Gods before me. There are no other Gods but me. There are no other Gods but one and that one is the "I am" of your being and of my being and of his being and her being and its being. And now even though you are not in this room and the telephone call comes to me that you are sick or sinning or poor or dead, I must be alert enough to say, "That's a rumor, because I'm looking right at the image of God, and I know that God is the only identity of individual being."

Do you not see that only that constitutes an individual who is set apart from mortal belief? Do you not see that only an individual who has in some measure realized that God is individual identity, that each one is the child of God, and so that when the rumors come of sin, disease, death, lack, and limitation, we can say, "So what? What power is there in such rumors and beliefs? What power is there even if somebody accepts such things? I know not any. I'm not concerned what somebody else accepts or believes. What am I accepting?"

Now in the light of that let us everyday ask and knock and seek, but for more and more light. Let us remember that which was given to us recently — we can pray for anything we want in the world as long as its something not of `this world.' Never forget that. Never, never pray for anything that is of `this world' because you can't demonstrate it spiritually. Pray all you want, ask all you want, seek all you want, knock all you want — only be sure that it's for something is not of `this world.'

Now let us meditate. . . .

Now comes the shortest part but the most important part of this whole lesson. Why after all this was it necessary to meditate? Because not one bit of this was of any importance to anybody in the world except in the degree of the click or realization. It exists only in the realm of thought or statement or anything else you want until it becomes vital, alive, active, through realization. Do you see now that knowing the truth as we have been knowing it for an hour is but one part and the least part of the whole demonstration. The greatest part comes in the next minute when we stop our voicing of truth, go within and let God put the seal on it. When God places the seal on it by giving us a second of realization, a feeling of "It is done" or "I am on the field" then and then alone is the other 59 minutes worth while. So it is with your individual treatments. You may declare all of these things about every rumor or temptation that comes to you. You may go through all the routine of remembering, probably even memorizing every word of this but remember this that you have accomplished nothing for yourself or for the world until you have had God's seal placed on it in meditation, by an inner assurance — "It is done" — "It is well" — "I am on the field" — or a release.

You see, I would like to bring you release from the thoughts and the things of the world. Now, I can only bring — God can only bring you — God can only bring you a release from the thoughts and things of the world when you have consciously known this letter of truth and then gone within for the actual experience or consciousness of truth. It is not the words we say or think or write or read, but the consciousness of it that we attain in our meditation.

And so I say to you also, we could just as well have avoided this whole last 59 minutes by starting off the first minute with the meditation and then going home. Always remember that — that the only reason for reading books and having classes and hearing lectures is to lead up to the point of realization. But the day will ultimately come when we won't need the whole 59 minutes, we will take the 60th minute in the first minute and achieve the same result. Because the result is achieved not by what we've said or heard but by the degree of realization of it — the click. Never forget that. With all of the truth knowing that takes place in your consciousness during the day or night, do not be satisfied with it until you have gone into meditation and gotten or received or achieved that inner release which says, "God is on the field."

8. Above and Beyond Thought or Thing

The nature of error in our writings makes it possible to understand the all-ness of God whereas, studying the all-ness of God would never enable us to get through error.

Let me illustrate that for you. I don't know of a single religion in all of the world that does not acknowledge that God is the only power. Every religion does that and because of that they have to acknowledge that God calls home his beloved ones, sometimes when they are only two, five, ten, or fifteen years of age. God gets weary sometimes or lonesome up there and he sends for his innocent little children to keep him company. You've heard ministers tell you at funerals, "This is the will of God. God is calling his loved ones home." You have seen people in terrible afflictions and heard that this is the will of God. The will of God is inscrutable. We can't see why this is, but God knows it's for our good. God is the cause of these violent acts: storms at sea, hurricanes, volcanoes. That's why insurance companies don't have to pay off on them. They are acts of God. Now, how does the church say that God is the only power in the face of all these things? By acknowledging that God is responsible for them. In that sense then, if you judge by appearances, you must acknowledge that there are sick people, sinful people, or dying people. You must acknowledge that there are accidents, that there are all kinds of natural disasters and man-made disasters and behind all of this you must acknowledge God if God is the only power. Now, there is no other way out of that dilemma. That is the way the church has taken it. God is the only power; therefore, God is calling his dearly beloved home.

Now, scripture very plainly states that death is an enemy. True, it is such a strong enemy that it is the last one to be overcome, but death is an enemy according to scripture. And not only that, the Master, God, declares that his mission on earth, the spiritual mission, is to heal the sick and raise the dead, to open the eyes of the blind, to open the ears of the deaf, and yet we are told that blindness and deafness and sickness and death is the will of God.

There have been spiritually illumined people on earth who have seen that there is no death and some who have even seen that there is no birth. There are some who have seen that there is no disease on earth, no reality to any of these negative appearances. In the beginning Gautama, the Buddha, founded his entire revelation not on what God is, but what error isn't. The revelation that came to him under that bodhi tree was, all of these appearances are illusion, are not reality, are not taking place in time or space, they are taking place only in a universal mortal concept.

Very little of that principle came to light in the following years, although there have been some wonderful mystics on earth, men who have attained conscious realization of God, conscious oneness with God, conscious union with God, and yet in their revelation, in their conscious oneness with God, they did not perceive that accusing God of these errors was making God responsible for them and making them real and so we have very little on the subject until the original *Science and Health*. In the original *Science and Health* it is made clear again, for the first time in centuries, that God is the only power and that these appearances of discord do not have reality. In one place Mrs. Eddy summed up all of these discords, lumped them together under the term mortal mind and said that mortal mind wasn't a thing. It was a term denoting nothingness. Some of her early students, and I happen to know one or two of them in Boston, were marvelous healers, without any great knowledge of religion. But, they were great healers by virtue of the fact that they had caught that one point, and whenever troubles were brought to them they could smile and say, "Mortal mind, meaning nothingness." They could turn away from it without reacting to it, without fearing it, without protecting themselves from it, just by that perception that whatever it is that appears in the nature of an evil person or condition can be lumped under that one term, mortal mind, and then the word mortal mind torn up by calling it a term, not a condition, not a person, not a thing, but a term denoting nothingness.

Now, just as this teaching was lost after the generation of Gautama Buddha, so has it been probably half lost in Western Religion. There are still some who catch that point of Western Religion, but not too many. In the days of Buddha the error was this, that those not close to the original master, Gautama, took the word illusion and externalized it. They said sin, disease and death is an illusion, but now we have something to get rid of. Oh yes, it's not measles or mumps. It's an illusion, but now let us get rid of the illusion. Whereas originally the meaning was, yes it's measles or mumps, but it is an illusion, which means it's a mental image of nothingness.

An illusion in thought, a mental image, has no substance, has no reality. It is merely an unfounded belief about something, a rumor. But, the Hindus from then until now call illusion, or maya, this world, and then they disregard it and either try to get rid of it by dying out of it or ignoring it. Well, India is not a good example of a true faith continued. But, modern religionists, many of them, made the same mistake. They got out of the habit of saying I have a cold, or flu or grip so, they would call and say, "I have an illusion. Will you help me get rid of it?" Or, they would call and say, "Will you protect me or give me protective work from the illusion? Will you do protective work for me?" Why, a practitioner could be so busy in Boston on Wednesdays and Sundays that he would have nothing to do but sit all day and night and do protective work because of the enemy.

Now, all of this goes back to human, innate nature which really has two powers (the power of good and the power of evil, called the power of God and the power of Satan, or in philosophy good and evil, or in metaphysics the immortal and the mortal, always a pair of opposites) instead of seeing one as all and the other as a nothingness, an illusion, a maya, a false sense of something, an ignorance of something.

Now, if you could perceive the nature of an illusion, for instance, if you could look out of the window and see the sky sitting on the mountain and know that it is not happening out there, it is happening in your thought, in your false sense of sight, you wouldn't be afraid to climb to the top of the mountain for fear of running into the sky. Or, up until 1492, had they known the nature of illusion, they would have perceived that the sky doesn't settle down on the water out there about eight miles, that that is not an externalized, physical condition, but a mental image in thought, nowhere existing except in limited vision of that which is. Now, we either have to make statements like "God is all" and then when we are faced with appearances of discord just keep on saying God is all" until we arrive at that conviction or inner realization or else we have to use our powers of thinking, contemplation, until we are able to lift ourselves into the conviction of God's all-ness. There is but one power and that is God, but God is not the author of death. God is not the creator of death. God is not the creator of accidents. God is not the creator of storms at sea. God is not the creator of volcanoes and tornadoes. That is absolutely fantastic. You would have to go back to an ancient God to believe any such thing. You would have to give up your beliefs which says God is love to believe there is anything loving about a ship going down in the middle of the ocean or an airplane falling out of the sky for any reason whatsoever, even for an inscrutable reason.

If you can outgrow that ancient concept of God, if you can even give up the desire that God somehow annihilate your enemies, then you can begin to perceive God or revelation of God and you no longer will battle sin, disease, death, lack and limitation. You will begin to understand the nature of error as an appearance, as a suggestion, as a presentation that has no concrete existence, no outlined form. Eventually, if you are not afraid to think about religion, and about God, and about this universe, if you have no superstitious scruples about thinking along religious lines, you will come to the ultimate realization of why there is error anywhere on earth and why it ever came on earth and what it is that continues it. You will find that it is fear. It is the fear of the word "I." I do not wish to be extinct and a little blister could become an infection that could kill me, I, Joel.

The only reason we fear unemployment is that we may starve to death or freeze to death. The only reason we don't like any form of sickness, no matter how mild it is, is that it might lead to death. There is only one error on all the earth and that is our own fear of our extinction, the little I, the me that would rather be 80 years of age than 60 on earth. Take all the men in the death houses in all the prisons that are fighting and sometimes spending fortunes to avoid the electric chair to stay in prison the rest of their lives.

There is only one reason, the fear of extinction. They know that the living is going to be worse than death, but at least it is going to be some form of "I" continuing, walking around in dungeons. They would rather have that "I" walking around in a dungeon than to face what may lie before it. Why is self-preservation the first law of nature? That gives you the whole secret of error, self-preservation.

We all want to preserve this sense of "I," even in its miseries. People are lying in bed at 80, 90, and 100 years of age, living dead, but they won't let themselves go. No. They are going to cling to that false sense of "I," even though it accomplishes nothing on earth but lying in bed the rest of its days. I am not saying that as if they could help it, because they can't help it any more than we can help it and there isn't anybody in this room that isn't doing the same thing. No exceptions, we are all clinging to a sense of "I" and it is that "I" that we want made comfortable. It is that "I" that we would like to glorify by being president, or being dictator or by being this, that, or the other thing. It is that "I" that we wish to glorify by seeing our name in print or something else. It is that false sense of "I" that we are catering to, that we are worshiping, and that we are feeding and that we are clothing. So long as there is this false sense of "I," there will be the fears about it and that will lead to every error there is on earth because in proportion as we would lose our fears, the errors themselves would disappear.

The illustration of that is this: "I" is God. And God is self maintained and self sustained and the minute you give up your concern for the false sense of that "I", it goes right along enjoying itself, prospering itself, drawing to itself everything and everyone that it needs for its unfoldment. But, entertaining the false sense of "I" sets up a fear, a fear of its ultimate extinction but also a fear of temporary discomfort. That is why in the Hindu scriptures it is said that you must face disgrace with the same feeling that you face honors, with utter indifference because the fame and the disgrace are about a false sense of you, not of you. You neither deserve fame nor ill-fame. You deserve nothing. God is the only one. And so, as you could give up resentments, as you could stop resenting thrusts at the false sense of yourself, you wouldn't be meeting any.

In the same way, as you could give up any desire for recognition, for honor, you would be losing that false sense of self and there would be less of sinful desires and less of disease and an absolute impossibility of death. But as long as there is a sense of self that welcomes recognition and fights rumors about itself and gossip and slander, that is the catering to a false sense of "I".

The nature of error, you see, reveals the nothingness of all these evils in the world, the non-power of them, by very virtue of the fact that their only claim to existence is having a false sense of "I" to exist in and act upon and through. Without that false sense of "I", where would error be? Where would it be if there were no "I" to be sick, where would sickness be? If there were no "I" to sin, where would sin be? If there were no "I" to die, where would death be? It would be in the same place that sound would be if there were no one out there to hear it. It just wouldn't be sound. It wouldn't be there. And so, there would be no death if there weren't person to die.

Then, isn't the error that sense of person that says, "I am separate and apart from God, that there is a me separate and apart from God?" Isaiah saw all of this. He said, "There is no God, but me." In other words, there is only one God, therefore there can only be one me. He saw and felt and realized no selfhood apart from God. He couldn't speak of himself as man because that false sense, that separate sense of selfhood, had disappeared.

9. Nature of God as Love

The start of the spiritual life is a state of self deception. The spiritual path seems to promise peace, joy, freedom to one's self. It appears to offer God's grace to you and to me. We confidently believe that evils will not come nigh our door. That ills will miraculously fade and abundant good will ever be our measure.

Hopefully we enter the way feeling ourselves set apart from other men — free of their trials, temptations, and fears. Truly this must be paradise in which men walk as though angels — God inspired, God protected, God sustained. And for a while it really seems as if all this were true. We appear to flourish by our understanding. Our cup runneth over by our spirituality. In other words, we are puffed up. Here Satan enters in the form of ourselves with desire for greater light, higher vision, a more saintly bearing. Our self would add to our self more of God, more of good, more of grace. Seeking to retire even more from the world of men to have more of God, to commune more with Him, to feel more of His presence. Our self is in the ascendancy but must diminish. And here the long nights of struggle begin. Today feeling high in spirit as if the world were ours. Tomorrow doubting and wondering. Next day plunged into an abyss convinced that God has forsaken us. But why? Have we not lived a chaste life in the path? Have we not meditated and communed? Have we not sought to show what good things follow those who walk with Him. Why hast though forsaken us when we would have more of Thee? Has not our very goodness, obedience, diligence, earned for us more of Thy good? So seeks the self to glorify itself by earning more of God. So seeks the self to satisfy itself. Always the self would draw to itself more of Him to the glory of the self. Prideful self must puff itself even in His light. The seesaw of spiritual pride and self dejection goes on and on, up and down, and sometimes around, until realization dawns. Up to now, we have been glorifying the self with God. Spiritual grace has made us vein with pride in our spiritual progress, our spiritual fruitage, our spiritual development and rewards. The self may not advance through Spirit. The self may not be glorified or pleased with itself. The self may not adorn itself with gifts of light, but must don sackcloth and ashes until its extinction. Thus begins the pain and poverty of spiritual progress. Thus the dying daily starts within oneself. The way is straight and narrow. The dying self is not content to peacefully pass away but must resist with every bit of remaining strength succumbing to its inevitable fate. The self will not easily or quietly yield, and every day's delay is agony to the soul that would surrender itself to God. Only in the final black night is self extinguished and God reveals Itself. In this light, no self glorifies itself by God contact. No self shows forth the fruitage of the Spirit. No self remains.

You see, all through this period of development it would seem as if we as individuals were really becoming more spiritual, more honest, more moral, more happy. And for a long while it is that sense that we ourselves are something better than our neighbors. It is only when in some deep problem that God reveals Itself to us as our self, that there is no longer a self to be proud of anything, or to take pride in its accomplishments, or to glory over this, that, or the other thing — because that which is now our Godself is the only self living in its own expression. And that which was our humanness is extinct. There is no more personal pride. And you can tell that. You can tell it the moment it comes to you, you no longer have judgment, or criticism, or condemnation for the other man's sins or faults because you understand them. And your prayer always is that their eyes be opened, that they may be awakened, and above all things that they may be forgiven for their ignorance, not punished, nor held in punishment to their own offenses.

10. The Garden of Eden — Neither Good Nor Evil

There are two questions asking, "How did the thought of good or evil come about in the Garden of Eden?" And my answer is, "How do you know that the thought of good or evil came about in the Garden of Eden? Have you experienced it. Why don't you wait a year and practice the lesson that we are having here tonight and then see whether the belief of good or evil ever did spring up, because up to this minute you have no knowledge that it did. None whatsoever. So you're asking a suppositional question. And nobody could answer that. You will be able to answer it within a year. All you have to do is to begin tonight to practice this lesson."

When you leave here and go to your room, think for a few moments on the vital problems that are disturbing you — your own or your children or your grandchildren. And as you think about them ask yourself, "Are these conditions good or evil? And who said so? Who told me that these were good or evil?" And then remember you are part of a class receiving instruction. And the instruction that you are receiving is that there is neither good nor evil. And in spite of all the beliefs about it, it can't make it any more real than if you were to believe that two times two are five. If somebody were to give you two objects and two objects and left you alone in a room with them for a whole year, you couldn't get five out of them. It's an impossibility regardless of what your belief would be to get more than four out of two times two. Because a belief can't make anything so. And all we want to know at this moment is — Is this sin evil? Is this disease evil? Now the question is also asked, "Did God create it?" Did God create evil? I think you know better than that. If God created eternality or immortality — if there is nothing in God that defileth or maketh a lie — certainly God didn't create evil. If God didn't create evil who did? Or have you been entertaining a belief in good and evil? If you are who gave you that belief? You don't know now but you will know a year from now. You'll know exactly where it came from. But at this time you can know nothing more than this — that there is neither good nor evil. That the entire first chapter of the Bible is dedicated to revealing a state of consciousness of spiritual perfection, wholeness, completeness, without material processes.

And that there is no other creation until someone accepts a belief in good and in evil. And then what happens? The very moment that a belief in good and evil is accepted, we are outside the kingdom of harmony — the kingdom of God. And the moment we are out there what happens? A material creation takes place.

Now what created the second chapter of Genesis creation? The belief in good and evil. And everything that's reported in the second chapter of Genesis as having been created was created out of the belief of good and evil. It is not a God creation. It is not a spiritual creation and it is not subject to God, and it is not subject to the law of God, and it is not subject to the government of God, and that is why spiritual healing

31

cannot take place on a human plane. Spiritual healing can only take place when you have stopped thinking of the person and the disease and the condition and the belief and the claim, and returned to Eden where there is neither good nor evil, where there is only God — Spirit — wholeness and completeness. No one can ever be a spiritual healer who works from the standpoint of effect — who prays from the standpoint of trying to correct something in the Adam world. Because if you succeeded you'd just have a pleasant dream instead of an unpleasant one. If you succeeded in improving this picture you would only have good materiality instead of bad materiality. You still would not be near the kingdom of God.

You for a brief moment in meditation, sit back close your eyes and begin to realize this — that out there external to me there is nothing good and nothing evil. There is only the presence of God — the universe of God's creating — the Spirit of God indwelling. This is a spiritual universe peopled with children of God. Now out there we can see some people who we consider evil. Don't be afraid to look at them. Don't be afraid to see them right in front of you. Whoever it is, wherever it is or they might be that you consider evil. And stop to think if everybody on Earth thinks them so — if there aren't just as many people or more who may consider them perfectly wonderful people. And then see whether or not they are evil or whether you have accepted an evil concept of them. Remember that if they were evil in and of themselves that is the way the world would see them.

Try to look at the roses of which this city has such an abundance and try to realize now that there are no good roses just as there are no evil roses. There are just roses. If you like them have them by the millions if you want. They have beauty. They have grace, perfume, form, and we like them. That doesn't say they're good, it just says that they're enjoyable. So let's have them. Ah, but here comes the next person who says, "No, no, no. Those flowers give me rose fever." How can that be? Now let us reverse this and see these roses as neither good nor evil but just roses. Just see them as partaking of the nature of God. Neither good nor evil but beautiful, colorful, harmonious, enjoyable.

Let's turn from roses or any other form of flowers and let's see our animals. Is there such a thing as a good dog or a good cat? No. There are dogs and there are cats. If they have any qualities of good we imbue them with those qualities. There are other people that cannot find that good in them. So let us now withdraw our concepts and agree there is neither good nor evil in dogs and cats, there are just dogs and cats. They may be beautiful and they may be friendly and they may be protective and they may be desirable, and we may love to have them around. But that's it. We are not going to call them good, we are not going to call them evil, we are going to call them only, creatures of God. You would be surprised when you begin to take this attitude for cats and dogs to find that every cat and dog in the world will be looking for you and wanting to be petted by you. Why? Because you are no longer expressing an opinion about dogs and cats, you are expressing the truth — they are dogs and cats of

God's creating. And that's what they are and that's what they want to be. And they want to be no more than that and no less than that, but they want to be understood for that. This is a dog and this is a cat and this is the creature that God has made. And the only qualities present are not good qualities or bad qualities — God qualities.

And then let us turn to these humans. Those we like and those we dislike. Those we trust and those we distrust. And let us, you and I, withdraw from them all our previous concepts. And let us say, "You are neither good nor bad. You are the man of God's creating or the woman of God's creating. You are neither good nor bad. Whatever qualities you have are God's qualities. I will not vest you with any qualities. I will not pin my concepts on to you. I will see you as you are. Adam and Eve of God's creating. Pure undefiled in God's grace." Watch the miracle of human relationships when you begin to withdraw your concepts of the men and women in your life and begin to agree that they are not good and they are not bad, but that they are children of God, and that the qualities of God constitute their true being.

There is neither good nor evil. That is our basic truth. There is neither good nor evil. All there is is God and God being. But stating that in and of itself does not always bring about the change that we would expect. So there must be this further step of inner communion which results in the Spirit being released. Now watch this, you've all had experience trying to meditate and I'm sure that most of you have found it difficult and probably still have some difficulties with it. Now watch the difference as you sit back to meditate and first think of anything you like and with your eyes closed look at it and begin to realize this is neither good nor evil. Neither good nor evil. Just man or dog or cat or woman. This is neither good nor evil. And watch how quickly your thought settles right down in to peace. Because I discovered something. Nobody can think unless they're thinking about something good or evil. There isn't anything you could think about unless you give it the title of good or evil. You can only be at peace. You can contemplate let us say some beautiful flowers. No, they're not good or evil, but they're surely beautiful. And you're already at peace.

Look at a person or look at a home, look at an animal and agree — neither good nor evil here just the Grace of God the Peace of God. And see how quickly you settle right down into meditation. It is almost accomplished in the twinkling of an eye as long as you have nothing good or evil to think about. Nothing that you hate or fear or love. Just something that you contemplate without emotion. And you see it is the good and evil that arouses the emotion. When it is neither good or evil there is no emotion. There is only what we might call pure joy — spiritual joy. See if you don't settle back quickly. See that. And you watch now as you learn to meditate that way looking at anything or anyone you like but withdrawing your concepts of good and evil. Settle into that peace and it'll only take a few minutes until the peace that passeth understanding begins to touch you and you feel that presence within you and sometimes even hear the Word Itself or hear a message of release, of assurance, of freedom. And in between comes that passage "Thy grace is my sufficiency in all things." And see how your thought is taken away from all persons and conditions. You're completely released in the knowledge that you have no need of persons and conditions. You have no fear of persons or conditions and that too, settles you into your peace. "Thy grace is my sufficiency in all things," and immediately the physical or material bondage that you were in to person or circumstance or condition just evaporates — "Thy Grace" — free of all human ties.

And so it is that all of the discords of this life — having to earn one's living by the sweat of the brow, having to bring forth children with pain and labor, all of this came with knowing good and evil. All of this ends when we no longer know good or evil and puts us right back there in the Garden of Eden — God maintained, God sustained, God equipped, the wisdom of God, the life of God, the love of God, the flow of God and nothing else but that.

11. The Infinite Way, Origin and Principle

The beginning of all this work was the realization that healing work is not based on a power that destroys sin, disease, death, lack, or limitation. It is not based on two powers struggling with each other. And as revelation followed revelation, unfoldment followed unfoldment, this ultimately came — the entire human scene is the operation of one power over another — one power destroying another — one power overcoming another. Always resorting to some power to do something to some other power. And when metaphysical and mental healing began it began on that basis of truth — overcoming error, the immortal destroying the mortal, the real doing away with the unreal, so that the two, good and evil, were still perpetuated.

Now come with me for just a few minutes in to an inner unfoldment — an inner stillness in which you are not going to resort to any power to do any thing. You are going to resist not evil. You are going to be still and let evil do anything it wants. You will not deny it. And you will not affirm. You will not seek God. You will not fear a devil. Sit at peace. Be still. In quietness and confidence shall be your strength.

Can you imagine the enormity of that statement?

In quietness...and confidence...shall be your strength. No struggle, no strife, no battle. Quietness and confidence. The Lord is my shepherd. He maketh me to lie down in green pastures. He leadeth me beside the still waters. He seteth a table before me in the wilderness. He performeth that which is given me to do. He perfecteth that which concerneth me. I shall not fear what mortal conditions can do to me. I and my Father are one. In Him I live and move and have my being. His grace is my sufficiency in all things.

Be still. You need not fight. The battle is not yours. Be still. Be still and know.

Where the Spirit of the Lord is there is liberty. Where the Spirit of the Lord is there is liberty.

No fight, no strife, no struggle — peace. Peace...peace...my peace give I unto thee. Not as the world giveth. Not as the world giveth.

Not a peace that comes from destroying your neighboring country — neighboring people. Not a peace that comes from having atomic bombs. Not as the world giveth, give I unto thee — my peace.

Nothing shall destroy thee. Nothing shall harm thee. For there is nothing but peace. The lion and the lamb shall lie down together.

Peace. Be still. Put up thy sword. Put up thy defense. Those who live by the sword will die by the sword — even a mental sword — put it up. Stop defending yourself. This is not power. This is not evil. Father forgive them, they know not what they do. In every prayer, in every meditation, in every treatment, remind yourself, "Put up thy sword." Don't argue. Don't refute. Don't defend. Don't protect. Put up that sword — mental sword — be at peace.

My peace give I unto thee. I shall not fear what mortal man can do to me for that's the belief, belief, belief, not power. And belief hurts only the believer. Put up thy sword. In quietness and confidence shall be thy strength. God's grace is thy sufficiency.

All right now that was the original revelation that started this whole career that resulted in the Infinite Way. The realization that you are still in the human world whether you heal with medicine or whether you heal with thoughts, you're still in the realm of physical healing. But the moment that you give no power to the condition — no power to the circumstance and understand that — in that moment you are at the point of spiritual healing, but you're also at the point of spiritual living because now you have no fear of the conditions of the world.

It's a very strange state of consciousness for the human to understand. I'm thinking now of a man who is a very great man in England, and this was just before World War II when things were pretty chaotic over there and the umbrella was still flying, and conditions were dangerous. And a man said to this great one, "You don't seem to be disturbed by the things that are threatening our country today or the world."

And this man answered, "My kingdom is not of this world." And you can imagine how that was misunderstood by everybody to whom it was repeated. As much as to say I don't care what happens to my country or to the world, but you know he didn't mean that. He meant this, which we're talking about, "My kingdom is not of this world," and so I cannot use the world's weapons. I must use the spiritual weapon which isn't a weapon at all — it's a realization.

And there came the second unfoldment that resulted in the Infinite Way — the word "realization."

The only treatment, the only prayer, the only meditation, the only weapon we have is that one word "realization." When you are in prayer or meditation, regardless of what you think, regardless of what thoughts come to you, you are only in the process until the moment of realization comes and in that moment of realization there is what we call healing or redemption, whatever the nature of the God's grace must be.

The words we speak are not power. The thoughts we think are not power. But if I sit in this quiet and I allow myself to think such thoughts as "peace be still" — "the victory is to be achieved not by might nor by power but by my Spirit." I'm not seeking for a power to destroy something. Oh no, thy grace Father, thy grace is my sufficiency. Thy presence is a lamp unto my feet. Thy peace passeth understanding. In thy presence is fullness of life.

As I sit contemplating these spiritual truths, which is a form of meditation, eventually I arrive at a place where thoughts do not come anymore, or perhaps I've thought all the thoughts along that line that I know. And so I just sit quietly, peacefully, and in a moment or two or three or four or five, I begin to feel this inner peace that is called realization. And that realization is the demonstration.

Now you see I haven't known any deep metaphysics. I haven't known any deep wisdoms. I haven't gone around knowing a lot of great knowledge that's hidden from the world. I have done nothing but take our Master literally at his word that I need not fight evil. I need only seek the kingdom or the inner peace and then all these things are granted unto me. That's the whole secret of this message.

You must know that if there is such an entity or identity as The Infinite Way and if it has spread around the world, it must have certain principles by which it is known, certain principles that identify it, certain principles that set it apart — and these are they. This really constitutes what we call the message of The Infinite Way. The Master taken literally at his word and then the development of a state of consciousness that enables us to live it.

12. Symbolism, Concepts

"Lean not unto thine own understanding. Acknowledge Him in all thy ways."

And so it is, that as we have in our homes or on our walls, some symbolic representation of a religious idea or ideal it can serve to remind us that we must think of God and spiritual things more often, and turn us more often to our realization of God, our demonstration of God. But if it goes beyond that to where we would accept any of these [religious icons] as really imaging forth God, or representing that which God is, we would then lose our demonstration because, first of all regardless of what degree of spiritual illumination you may attain, you will still not have the fullness of the Godhead bodily as your demonstrated mind. Now that doesn't mean that God the infinite isn't your intelligence, but at no time in your career can you embrace that infinity or you would be infinity itself. And therefore, any concept of God that you would entertain must be something less than infinity since you cannot embrace infinity.

Now, when you realize that, you come very close to being ready for the God experience. Certainly, you will never come to it before you realize that there is no possibility of knowing God. And that regardless of what you have read or heard, what you may think you know about God, it cannot be that. In the Infinite Way we talk a lot about the nature of God, and that's something quite different than talking about God. For instance, we do know the nature of God by the effect of God. In other words, after you have had God contact, you can know what the nature of God is by its effect upon you. But knowing the nature of God, and knowing God, these are two different things.

To prepare for the God experience it is necessary in the earliest stages to close one's eyes. And let us realize here and now, "If I could name it, it isn't that. If I could think it, it isn't that, because all I can think is something less than myself, and certainly I am not that."

Now, since I acknowledge that I, Joel, do not know God, and that with my thinking mind, my reasoning mind, I never can encompass God, for I'd be encompassing the infinite in the finite. Now, in acknowledgement of that, I open myself and say, *"Father, I cannot know you, but you can know me. I cannot encompass you, but you can encompass me."*

True, I and the Father are one, but the Father is greater than I. And that's a mystery that you understand with the very first God experience.

"I and the Father are one, but the Father is greater than I. Father, reveal thyself. Speak Lord, thy servant heareth."

And now, having completely cleared yourself of all concepts about God, all beliefs about God, all theories about God, or superstitions, concepts, symbols — you learn to sit receptive, awake, and alert— as if you actually expected God to walk right into your consciousness.

And it isn't impossible. And that still doesn't mean that you will know God or be able to describe God, but you will be able to say, "I have experienced God. I have felt the presence. I have felt the power." And you can know it by its effects.

Now, in our work in the Infinite Way, this is a necessary step because it leads to some other steps which in their turn lead to the ability to heal. Because if I do not know God, and who can with this mind, and I agree to that and I am receptive, I will sooner or later receive or have an experience which will satisfy me that God has either spoken to me, or revealed Himself to me, or made the presence and power available. There will never be any doubt once it happens even though there may be a dozen near experiences before that which may make you say, "Now was that the experience?" It probably wasn't. Because usually when it comes, it comes with such distinct force or power or gentleness or realization that you know it so, but you know it so thoroughly that it becomes sacred and you don't mention it, it's secret.

If you find yourself talking about it then be assured that that wasn't it. Because nobody who has the experience would risk its loss by casting a pearl before swine — casting their greatest demonstration before the unprepared thought. No, there is nobody ever, who has had that experience, who will talk about it, unless they find themselves in the company of those whom they know by the demonstration of their lives, have also attained.

In other words, as you travel here and there you will recognize a mystic or you will recognize a God realized person. You won't have to speak to them and they won't have to speak to you. Before you separate from them there will be a look in your eyes and a look in theirs and you will instantly identify yourselves, and then at that time or some other time you will find yourself in the position of exchanging experiences. But other than that you could no more be tempted to talk about it than you could be tempted to talk about the most intimate details of your own life.

13. Individual Discovery of Truth

I suppose we could say that what I have been saying to you represents my own discovery of truth. I don't mean my invention of it but my own way of coming to the discovery and realization of it. And that part of this work of the Infinite Way is to help others make a discovery within themselves of truth.

You can see that it would be fatal just to open the books and read them and swallow everything and just say, "That's it." — and then go around quoting Joel and proving that that's it. That's really not the nature of the message of the Infinite Way. That is why we're not organized or rather it's one of the reasons we're not organized.
We're not prepared to say that, "This is the truth, the whole truth, and nothing but the truth, and we hope that you never read anything else."

This is more or less an impulse that there is within me to share with those who are led to me, my discovery and those things which I discovered, but above everything to reveal to them *how* I discovered it so that they may make these discoveries themselves.

Now as you know, I did not begin to perceive the nature of truth until I learned about meditation. I did have the spiritual experience, I had many of them, and I was doing spiritual healing work but I did not know the nature of truth. I could've quoted some things out of books but that was a long, long way from having any knowledge of truth. You might really say that I was living on quotations, and living on quotations is not a healthy diet. They're helpful in the early stages but that's all.

Now when I learned the secret of meditation that is when I began to learn the secret of life. And through meditation I have discovered things which are in the writings and which are in our class work but which can only be valuable to you when you discover them and realize them within yourself.

For instance, I might quote to you one statement which should make all other scripture obsolete and unnecessary.

"I and my Father are one. Son thou art ever with me and all that I have is thine."

Now you know if you really know that you have ended your search for truth, and you have ended your search for God, and you need no scripture, you need no teachers, you need nothing — you have it all. And yet you know as well as I do that those words have been in the Bibles for hundreds of years and still here we are studying, meditating, pondering... Why? Even though you were to agree with the Master that that is the absolute truth — *"I and the Father are one."* — you are still far from the demonstration of it, the realization, in fact you may be just as far as you were before you even heard those words. It takes more than knowing words. It takes actual experience. I think it's in the first chapter of "Living the Infinite Way" that I have said that the Infinite Way is not another message on truth but the experience of God. And that's what it is because that's what it leads to. Reading the books isn't an experience of God but reading the books can lead to it if you follow through.

Now this is very important to know what I've just said because I'm going to lead to a point that probably is the modern language way of saying that, *"I and the Father are one, and all that the Father hath is mine."* And yet, it says something beyond that. Now this too, was a discovery, and this too was a revelation, and it was a revelation that came to me through meditation. And that is why meditation plays the important part in our work that it does. I believe you can learn anything you want with your mind but I do not believe that you can demonstrate any spiritual truth until you rise above the level of thought and mind into the intuitive spiritual faculty. And, so far, there is no way known on Earth of accomplishing that except by means of meditation.

Yes, it does come to some by a divine grace. For some unknown reason the finger of God reaches out and touches some people and there they are. They're in the full and complete spiritual consciousness without ever having taken the steps that we take leading up to it. There have been many such people. One of our happiest and yet unhappiest of men was one of those — that was Walt Whitman. Walt Whitman was just a miserable man like the rest of us when in some unknown way for some unknown reason, except perhaps that there was an inner longing, the finger of God touched him and he entered the realm of spiritual awareness. What kept him miserable afterward was that he had to live in two worlds, and living in two worlds is a difficult thing.

Now for the rest the finger of God touches us just to the point of giving us an inner hunger — an inner dissatisfaction. Sometimes that hunger and dissatisfaction becomes so great that we become diseased — physically or mentally or morally or financially. And when that gets deep enough in us a cry goes out of us, "Oh God, oh God, oh God! Is there a God?" And that's usually the beginning of wisdom because from there on we are very apt to follow some way until we arrive.

Those who are led to the point where you are today — even those of you who are just beginning on this way — you are ready for the experience of meditation and those who have it must prepare themselves for deeper forms of meditation until they arrive at an actual communion with God. Communion is meditation carried to a far deeper degree. Communion is that point of meditation where you actually come into the experience of tabernacling with the spirit of God within you — where it is even possible to have conversations with God. Or where it is possible to sit and receive these beautiful impartations — sometimes in words or thoughts, sometimes just in awareness, just in sensing. But at least it is that point of communion where there seems to be a flow between God and me — and an incoming and an outgoing, a turning and a returning, an inner communion, a sweetness, a gentleness, a peacefulness — sometimes that transcends all words and thoughts.

And, of course, that's not the stopping place. Because as one reaches there one eventually transcends that to where one's own self completely disappears and there's nothing left but God. It's a completely pure state of being and in those moments one is not only aware of themselves, one may well be aware of themselves out in the grass, or in the trees, or in the birds, or in the sea. It is a sense of self that has no finite or corporeal limitation. It's not an imaginary state because if it were you could bring it on at will. It isn't anything one can bring on or induce. It is something that automatically comes at a certain state of realization and revelation.

Now it was through such experiences that the classes which now form the books "Living the Infinite Way," "Practicing the Presence," and "The Art of Meditation" have come. You must remember that none of those books were written as books. You must remember that in my whole life I've never written a book. All of these which are in print now and seems to be some authors writing, actually were just messages that were spoken as this one is being spoken and was later printed on paper. None of my works were ever written as a book is written. None were ever thought out in advance. None ever had notes drawn up, or a outline or a diagram. None ever had a subject or a way of formation. Every one of them came as this one is coming just out of meditation — and it's being taken down on a recorder and eventually it will be a book, or an article, or a monthly letter — it'll be in print somewhere and somebody will wonder when Joel gets the time to write all these books. Well, fortunately he doesn't need time because he doesn't write them. Now it was in these meditations and as a result of this work that this particular unfoldment came. And while it appears all through all of the Infinite Way writings it came to a head in the First Honolulu Closed Class — it was the subject of the first and second night.

The first night was "The Nature of God as I" but the second night was "The Nature of Individual Being" — your being and mine. Now this constitutes — and as I say you'll find this all the way back in my earliest writings — but this constitutes one of the major premises that every student of the Infinite Way must learn even if at first they learn it only intellectually, and then later discern it spiritually.

And that is this: You are not man. And you are not woman.

You are not an effect. And you are not creation.

You are *I*.

And that is why when you name yourself that is the name you give yourself — "I". And even if you say Mary Jones after it, it's understood that you have first said "I".

That's why legal documents say that — "I, Mary Jones", and so on. "I" am not Mary Jones. I am "I" but I give myself the name Mary, Bill, Joel...

But always remember this, "I am *I*." And that's your true identity. And because of this you cannot receive anything even from God. Now here you have a major premise of the message of the Infinite Way. There's no use of praying to God for anything even if you could because you can't get it. The nature of my Being is *I*, and *I* is infinite.

"I and the Father are one, and all that the Father hath is mine."

That has nothing to do with the future tense. That has nothing to do with whether or not I'm good, bad, or indifferent. That has to do with the real nature of my Being. It has to do with, *"Ye shall know the truth and the truth will make you free."*

And the truth is, "I am *I*."

Moses gave it to the world, *"I am that I am."*

"I am" is the nature of your individual Being and that is why we have scriptural passages that show you how to live from that basis. *"Cast your bread upon the waters."* It doesn't say a word about pleading or begging for bread. It says, *"Cast your bread."* All the way through scripture you can find proof that good flows out from our being it does not flow to our being. If you wish to see the miserable lives that some people live because they're sitting around waiting for love to come to them. And others are waiting for friendship to come to them. And others are waiting for justice and for mercy to come to them. And they wait and they wait and they beg and they plead and they pray and it doesn't come. And if only they knew that there's only one way in which they can ever demonstrate having love, abundance, mercy, justice, goodness — and that's to give it out. Express it. Let it flow out. Cast your bread upon the waters.

"I and my Father are one and all that the Father hath in mine. Son thou art ever with me and all that I have is thine."

Now you will remember ... our lesson the on 58th Chapter of Isaiah in which we learned that it's no good to sit around and say these things and pray these things but that you have to act them out. And so I learned by meditation and then by actual demonstration that the fullness of the Godhead is in me. That God has fulfilled Himself as my individual being and I can demonstrate

it in proportion to my ability to live it. So that if I have but a few coins today and I accept this truth and am willing to part with one or two of them — to share it with someone who has still less — or if I have no coins but if I have merely this awareness of my identity and I'm willing to sit and pray or realize that truth for my fellow man, for my friends, for my neighbors, for my enemies — if I'm only willing to know the truth if that's all I've got — cast *that* bread upon the water.

Or if I can find some way to be a friend. If I can find some way of expressing forgiveness. If I can find someway of being more just, more merciful. In other words, if I can accept the Messianic message that, *"Thou seest me, thou seest the Father that sent me."* — even though the invisible is greater than the visible — nevertheless, *"Thou seest me, thou seest the Father that sent me."*

And I can begin in any given moment to act out that way of life by loving, sharing, forgiving, cooperating, being more just, being more merciful, being more kind. If I can begin in some measure to do that I begin the demonstration of my harmony.

Be assured of this — God has not created His own image and likeness and left it blank of anything. The image and likeness of God does not lack for anything. The image and likeness of God, God's own manifestation of Its own Being, hasn't got a lot of money and no health, or a lot of health and no money. The image and likeness of God hasn't got kindness, and justice, and mercy, but otherwise full of sin, sickness, and death. The image and likeness of God, or that *I* which I am, the Infinite Spirit Itself in individual manifestation and expression — that is the embodiment of all that God is and I am He.

That is a revelation of truth but it is not a demonstration of truth. The demonstration follows the acceptance and acting upon of that truth. And sometimes it is a slow process after we have accepted that because remember to all appearances we're sick and sinning mortals. To all appearances we're aging and dying humans. And so we are always violating appearances when we accept the truth about our own being — our own inner spiritual being. And so it is that we have to often have to close our eyes and realize this, "I'm not claiming Father, that a human being, a mortal, is divine. What I'm claiming is that a human being or a mortal must die to that seeming sense of self and realize that God Itself is Spirit but since God is all, God is infinite being even when it's individually expressed. I'm not claiming any truth for my mortalness, my mortality, or my human identity — I'm acknowledging that in this search for truth I'm attempting to die daily to my humanness — not spiritualize it. I'm trying to die daily to it — I'm trying to surrender it in the realization that God is infinite being and constitutes individual being, spiritual being, incorporeal being, invisible being, the being that I am.

Then as I ponder that and receive that inwardly I begin to understand the nature of the revelation of God. Now do you know why it is said, *"I am the way, the truth, and the life"* because that's what it means — *"I am the way, the truth, and the life."* Do you know what it means when it says — *"I will never leave you nor forsake you."* Why not just sit still for a minute and try to get rid of I? Just try to run away from it

44

— try to drown it — try to get anywhere, where I isn't. And you'll see why it is also said, *"If I make my bed in hell thou art there. If I mount up to heaven thou art there. If I walk through the valley of the shadow of death thou art there."* Why? Because I am there. I am here and I am there and I am everywhere. *"Lift up the stone and I am there."*

And I is God. I is infinite being. I is Self completeness. And so we have in the message of the Infinite Way a whole teaching on the subject of Self completeness in God and its spelled with a capital 'S'. It doesn't mean that we humanly are complete or perfect or self contained or self maintained — on the contrary, as human beings just look how we suffer and lack. But in putting off that selfhood and surrendering it and acknowledging that the *I* of my being can never leave me nor forsake me — as I was with Abraham so I am with you — I will never leave you nor forsake you. And then we come to that miracle, miracle, miracle teaching of God which is accepted wholeheartedly in the Infinite Way.

"I have meat."

No don't go to the city to get me any meat, *"I have meat that ye know not of."*

I am the wine of life. I am the bread of life. I am the resurrection. And that I will never leave me nor forsake me. And where I am, *I* is. For I is the true nature of my being, and I is my meat, and I is my wine, and my water, and my bread. I is the staff of life to me. I is my high tower, the rock on which I'm founded. I is my hiding place. I live and move and have my being in God — in the *I* that I am. God is my fortress and I hide in that fortress which I am. God is my high tower. Nothing by any manner of means can reach me, assail me, or injure me, because I am and beside me there are no powers to do any injuring. For I alone is power. I is bread, I is meat, I is wine, I is the resurrection. And if we secretly and silently always lift up the I — for if I be lifted up I shall draw all men unto me — and if I lift up the I in me silently and secretly, for remember this, and I give you this again and again and again . . . never forget this — this is Matthew, sixth chapter — *"Take heed that you do not your alms before men to be seen of them. Otherwise, ye have no reward of your Father which is in heaven."*

And don't think for a minute that that isn't a spiritual law — that the good we do publicly, the benevolences we do publicly are of absolutely no value beyond whatever praise we get from man whose breath is in his nostril. But our spiritual reward, our spiritual recognition lies in the fact that there is an I at the center of our being that knows what we're doing, thinking, and acting. And It, It performs for us so that what we do in secret is shouted from the housetops.

14. The God

Now we have learned first of all that there is this God and that it's ever available right where we are in any circumstances. Don't forget that it's just as available when we're going through the fire, when we're going through the floods, when we're going through the hurricanes, when we're going through the valley of the shadow of death — it's just as available. Don't turn your back on it because you're in a problem. That's the time to reach out harder than ever.

And we've learned that it is God that worketh in you. And so when the going gets very tough that's the time to relax not the time to tighten up, that's not the time to get fearful, that's not the time to get tensed and strained. That's the time to relax and realize, "I don't have to do this." It is God that worketh in me. It is not the whirlwind. It's not the hurricane, the storm, that reflects God, it's the still small voice. It is the gentle God. And so we come to that final word. From Genesis to Revelation we have God and the presence of God and the might of God and the power of God and the strength of God. And there we come to a word that defies definition or analysis or interpretation even. It's a word that you have to take, or a term that you have to take just as it is without any explanations — without any appeal to the reasoning mind to understand it. For the more you try to understand it the less you'll have of it. The more you can accept God without question, without any desire to analyze or understand it, the more of it you will have. The more you try to mentally probe the less you will have.

Scripture tells us that there are four temporal kingdoms using metals as a base but we know that it means forms of matter. And that these four temporal kingdoms will be destroyed. And then it tells us that these will be destroyed by a rock that is carved out of the side of a mountain without hands. That's pretty nearly ridiculous as you can get — a rock carved out of the side of a mountain without hands will fall on the four temporal kingdoms and crush them. Well you see even though you could not analyze such a statement or humanly reason it out still you can spiritually discern that there is that which is invisible and infinite — which takes from all material form its power so that in our consciousness we understand that the consciousness is not in the form but in the invisible Creator of the form. Now that statement doesn't mean that the world is going to do away with gold or silver or brass or atomic energy — it doesn't mean that at all. It means that God is going to take the destructive elements out of the forms of this world and govern them. Now you have already seen that done for instance in the case of electricity where the mind of man governs electricity and its uses and its activities — harnesses it for man's purpose. The mind does that. In the same way right now you are witnessing that atomic force is being harnessed and some day will be harnessed not to destroy man but to serve man and so the destructive force will be out of atomic energy and atomic energy will be a gentle little lamb governed by the mind of man — the *mind* of man. That very rock on which our life is based — the mind — which has no material form and yet it's the source of our intelligence or the seed of it or the avenue of it. That mind will harness every bit of this atomic power and eventually atomic power will be just as gentle a lamb as electricity is when it's properly hooked up. And they will be servants of man not destructive elements but constructive elements — servants of the mind of man.

And so it will be that one of these days you will find that every form of matter — take gold — gold which today dominates and rules man. It buys men's souls. There isn't a day of the week when men and women aren't selling their souls for gold or the equivalent of it. It's gold or its equivalent money that governments are using in this attempt to destroy each other or conquer each other. Money which is in that sense a devil will some day become just a pliant little thing in our fingers that we ourselves will use and have complete dominion over and it will never be able to buy us or bribe us but we'll be able to use it not to hold on to but to transfer and use for our purpose. Gold will be tamed so that one of these days it will be nothing more or less than an instrument for our use just like street car transfers that we don't hold to have any value but transfer that we don't use to have any value so it'll be with dollar bills or pound bills. They will no longer be powers. The power of God will crush all power out of money as a force and it will become just a tool, just a servant that we can mold to our use.

And so it will be that one of these days you will find that every form of matter — take gold — gold which today dominates and rules man. It buys men's souls. There isn't a day of the week when men and women aren't selling their souls for gold or the equivalent of it. It's gold or its equivalent money that governments are using in this attempt to destroy each other or conquer each other. Money which is in that sense a devil will some day become just a pliant little thing in our fingers that we ourselves will use and have complete dominion over and it will never be able to buy us or bribe us but we'll be able to use it not to hold on to but to transfer and use for our purpose. Gold will be tamed so that one of these days it will be nothing more or less than an instrument for our use just like street car transfers that we don't hold to have any value but transfer that we don't use to have any value so it'll be with dollar bills or pound bills. They will no longer be powers. The power of God will crush all power out of money as a force and it will become just a tool, just a servant that we can mold to our use.

And so you are going to find one day that all forms of matter are literally going to be under our feet. Germs, we'll have absolutely no fear of them at all. No fear of them at all. We will have conquered them. I'm thinking right now of an illustration where for many, many years the Eskimo of Alaska was subject to tuberculosis and to such a terrible extent that the medical facilities of Alaska were inadequate to care for it. And a law was passed permitting these Eskimo to be brought down to the states for treatment and you know that within just three years in three years time tuberculosis had been so conquered that they had been able to disband this sanitarium and give it up and have no further need for it. And the very little remaining tuberculosis that there is in Alaska is so little that the local authorities can handle it and take care of it. Those germs have become subdued. They're no longer the master of the Eskimo — they are the servants. They no longer master them.

So it is going to be with all forms of disease. Neither will the calendar. The calendar is one of the worst enemies of mankind there is because every time you tear off a page it's like tearing off a page of your life — there goes yesterday and fewer tomorrows. But that won't always be. That won't always be. A calendar will someday be man's friend and he will be in such complete control over time and the passing of time that time will have no effect on his mind or body whatsoever. And then instead of man dying out with either disease or age when his time comes to go into a higher experience he will make the transition the same as a child goes into the adolescent period. And the adolescent goes into the maturity period and then we go into the middle maturity period. So we will just on making transitions from one stage to another but that won't be while the calendar has power over us or while germs have power over us or while money has power over us or while bullets have power over us or bombs. It will be when we have dominion over the four temporal kingdoms.

When we through God — through the gentle Spirit — the still small voice will be able to say, "Thus far and no farther. Thou couldst have no power over me unless it came from the Father." Now you can begin to demonstrate that any day of the week that you like. You can't prove it to its fullness because that comes with time and maturity and experience. But you can begin as of this very moment. And just remember that within you there is this gentle God which may be called the still small voice or the voice of the Lord. And that as you develop the capacity to hear It — to listen to It — that It becomes dominion over everything on this Earth, above the Earth or beneath the Earth — the dominion that was given to us in the beginning when we were the image and likeness of God. Unto man was given dominion over these four temporal kingdoms. Everything in the Earth, everything in the sky, everything in the waters beneath the Earth, and everything in between, man was given God given dominion over. And the means of that dominion was the voice of the Lord. The voice of the Lord came to Adam and Eve. The voice of the Lord came to Moses to Abraham to Isaac to Jacob. The voice of the Lord gave Moses dominion over those horrible experiences in Egypt. The voice of the Lord does all of these things. There's a psalm, you can look it up in your concordance, I've forgotten which number it is but there is a psalm that is devoted almost entirely to the voice of the Lord and what the voice of the Lord does. And you'll be surprised what the voice of the Lord does. And in it you'll find also "he uttered His voice, the earth melted." That's the four temporal kingdoms. "He uttered His voice, the earth melted." All problems disappeared. All dominion over us was met and we were given dominion over these things. And so you see when people say that they haven't time for it, don't believe it any more than when they say they can't afford this or that. It's just a matter of what you wish to use your time for or what you wish to use your money for. We can afford anything and everything that we truly wish. And we can find time for everything for that which we really wish to find it for.

There was a period in my life when I was preparing for this work, not knowing that I was being prepared for it, when I could go through twelve solid years with an average of no more that three and a half hours sleep out of every 24 for twelve solid years, and I required no more sleep than that. And the reason was that I had to have all of those hours in use. In those twelve years I read the 1,500 hundred books that have become part of my consciousness. In those years I read some of those books through a hundred times from cover to cover. I really read. And all the time worked twelve hours a day as a practitioner doing the healing work and then for part of that time even went to the university to learn Sanskrit. So you see there is time because there are 24 hours in every day but how much do we wish to use it. If we wanted to use 20 hours out of 24 I can assure you that the grace of God would sustain us because it isn't sleep that we need, it isn't bed that we need, it's the grace of God we need. In the same way, we could get along on half the amount of food we consume because the grace of God would make up for the difference. We merely eat as much as we do because it's available and because it's tasty. Not because it's necessary. We can do with half if he have to and be just as healthy if not healthier for the grace of God has to be called upon when there's less of material reliance. Just as those as you already know who have come to Science and been told that they had to throw away their medicines. They got along without them. I know that the rest of the world wouldn't believe if it knew how many people there are who go 10, 15, and 20 years without a drop of medicine, without an aspirin, without a cathartic. The world would never believe such a thing because its physical setup is such that it must have aspirin, it must have cathartics, it must have this and it must have that as a minimum. And just think of all of us that you know about that have gone 10 or 15 or 20 or 30 years either with none or with so little that it's almost negligible. And then you'll know that it is possible to do away with that medicine cabinet because the grace of God supplants it.

I know sometimes there are some doctors who smirk about the subject of Religion Science or spiritual healing and like to tell about how they have a patient who's a Religious Scientist that sneaks to their office or had to have an operation or maybe they have two patients. But they forget about the tens of thousands who don't or that maybe even that one had to succumb once in a lifetime — that they don't stop to remember. That even though a Religious Scientist or a New Thoughtist or a Unity student or an Infinite Way student may once in a while have to resort through fear or family to material remedy compare it with the rest of the world and see how wonderfully the grace of God cares for us in place of material remedies and then you'll know what I mean when I speak of God. The God — that gentle presence which is the grace of God in our experience — how It carries us through.

And how when we learn to listen to It, hear It, and obey It, It finally gives us dominion over disease, over germs, over unemployment, over unhappy human relationships — gives us dominion. And then you'll understand why the day will come when that rock carved out of the side of a mountain without hands, that gentle God, that spirit of God within your consciousness will someday give you dominion over every element of human life including time, age, death itself — you will have dominion.

And so should the time come when you want to pass out of this plane of existence you will but not through being pushed out with some horrible disease but just by gently easing yourself out and into whatever experience lies before you because there is an experience that lies ahead of all of us. It is not going to be given to anybody on the face of the Earth to stay in this plane of life forever. If there were such a thing I'm sure that some of our ancient Hebrew and Christian and Oriental mystics would have done it because they lived their lives in full conformity to the will of God. Men like Moses, men like Enoch, Isaiah, Lao-Tzu, Buddha, Shankara — those men lived in accord with the laws of God and if it had been meant for anybody to stay on this globe forever they would have remained right here in physical form but they have all walked out of this form into whatever experience was ahead. And so will we when our appointed time comes. And it will be a way of transition, a transition into a higher plane of consciousness, one in which we will be freed of all the human ties, and human responsibilities, and human obligations. While we're here we can't shirk those but the day will come when we'll be released from them into the ability to walk our own way into the footsteps of God. And we'll do this remember through that thing called the God, or the Spirit of God in man, or the gentle Presence, or the still small voice. Call it whatever you will, it is within you, it is available to you through an inner hearing. It is available through you through an inner seeing.

Not the hearing of the outer ear, not the seeing of the eye, but through an inner seeing and an inner hearing and an inner feeling that Presence becomes alive. Now you may have to have four periods a day, and then six, eight, ten, twelve, twenty eventually. They may be one minute in length and some of them may be three and some may be ten minutes. Occasionally you may find one to last an entire hour in which you will sit in stillness and in quietness. "In quietness and in confidence shall be your strength."

The assurance that David had. The assurance when he said, "The Lord is my shepherd, I shall not want." That's the assurance that comes in stillness, in quietness, in peace, in tranquility. You develop that. The reason is that you have become separated from it by your centuries of human living. You have become separated from it through the belief that you had to earn a living by the sweat of your brow or keep a household with your physical strength. And now you're paying the penalty in a sense of separation from the still small voice that is always within you, ready, able and willing to speak to lead to direct. And now you have to go back. You have to retrace your footsteps to the Father's house. And I can tell you how — through the many, many periods a day in which you determine to take mastership of your clock and not let your clock tell you that you haven't time. But you tell the clock that you have 24 hours of time and loads of minutes in that 24 hours — count 'em up 24 times 60 and see how many you've really got there to set aside your periods, even if it were ten minutes before the rest of your household were awake, if it were five minutes after the men folk left the house, if it were five minutes before sitting down to that lunch or that dinner, if it were ten minutes before retiring, if it were just a few minutes waking in the middle of the night you would soon find that you are developing a capacity to be still, to be quiet, to be listening.

Nobody can tell you whether it will take you one week to receive the first intimation that something is happened or whether it might not be like in my case it took eight months. Eight months of more than a dozen periods set aside every day for meditation and still it took eight months before I had the first response. But then I had the second one a week later. And I had the third one probably two weeks later. And then a fourth one, one week later. And then gradually two in one week. And then eventually one every day and so on until now most of the time it is possible for me to sit as you see me here, get quiet for a minute and then all of a sudden have it come, and quickly, and quickly, and give me my message or give me my word or give me my Bible passage. Don't be surprised if I tell you that it was riding in the taxi between the hotel and here that these three Bible passages were given me that I read tonight. While we were riding in the taxi I had this Bible in my hands and I kept fidgeting with it and that's when it came. And then as I've sat here and turned within quietly every once in a while the message kept coming and coming and coming. It isn't a made up message. It's not memorized. It keeps coming in the degree that we turn in. Oh sometimes I have a little struggle because in my work where all day long and sometimes all night long I'm dealing with the problems of students and patients and some of them are pretty nasty problems. Sometimes you get pulled down off your high estate and then you have to build yourself back up again.

Sometimes people come into your experience that really pull almost everything out of you that you've got of a spiritual nature. That's all right you can rebuild it again and if it blesses them you don't mind it. But it does give you something to meet because you have to build back up again to where you were. We ought to go away much more than we do for this rebuilding.

And the Father within or the God, that's the voice. Now that voice, the word of God is quick and sharp and powerful. And when that voice utters Itself the Earth melteth. The whole four temporal kingdoms of the Earth melt. I have seen all forms of sin and all forms of disease melt away when that voice spoke within. I've seen all kinds of human wrongs made right when that voice spoke within. I've seen such power in our union relationships in the states — company and union — I've seen such things as you cannot imagine just as this same voice that gave me these Bible passages for this lesson tonight. That same voice. It's the voice of God. It's the gentle Presence. It's the calm. It's the inner assurance or tranquility. It's the grace of God. Call it any of these names but be sure of this that until you have it you are nothing. You are just aging human beings. You are just nothing.

Branches cut off from the tree that withereth. You are nothing until you have a contact within yourself. When you have you've made contact with living waters, the streams of life that renew and renew and renew just like they renew your plants, year by year, year by year, water does it. Only this is a living water that is within us. And it is that which gives us command over the four temporal kingdoms. It won't allow money to be our masters. It lets us be masters over money so that we can command whatever is necessary for our legitimate needs. It won't allow the body to master us forever. The God enables us to master not only our bodies but in as the experience of God and our practitioners even to govern the bodies of those that comes to us for help. It won't allow us to be made victims of the blitz as I brought out to you the other night. But you can walk the streets in the midst of the blitz and it will not come nigh your dwelling place if you're abiding in the secret place of the most high, if you are maintaining your contact with the inner Being, the Spirit of God in you. If you ignore it, if you refuse to make your contact with it, if you don't have the stamina to stick with it until it does take over your life you'll just have to do it in the next life. Some day or other you can be assured of this that every knee is going to bend, every head is going to bow to God. So if you put it off in this lifetime don't think that you can put it off in the next or the next or the next.

Someday you're going to have to look a clock straight in the eye and say you've got 24 hours of 60 minutes each and brother I'm going to use you. You are not going to use me. I am going to use you. And then it is that you'll find those five and ten minute periods when you can seat yourself and say, "Speak Lord, Thy servant heareth. My fate is not out there in the whirlwind, in the fire, in destruction. My fate is in the still small voice within me. And when he uttereth His voice in me the Earth of problems just melts away." And I'm going to learn to be still and I'm going to learn to listen. I'm going to develop the knack.

15. Soul - Mind – Body

What is it that has substance? What is it that endures forever? Laws of like begetting like. Deeds of love. The life that's renewed year by year. A tree becomes barren in winter, renewed in spring, fulfilled in summer. The life hasn't died just because some of its forms have changed expression. The life is there to renew itself forever and forever. The only things that are immortal and eternal are the invisible things of Spirit although each one of these is made tangible or evident in our experience in some form. But the form is never immortal as form. But the substance of it is always immortal. You see what confuses is really this — I think this is what has more metaphysicians fooled than anything else —

[Joel reads question from student] Have you any special reason for never saying in class that all there is to matter is an illusion of the senses?

Well, yes, I do have a very special reason. This isn't a fact. Matter is an indestructible substance. Matter is as indestructible as God and that's what has confused metaphysicians. They have been taught that matter is unreal. Matter can't be unreal because you can't destroy it. You can make it change forms but you cannot destroy matter. If you reduce it to molecules you'll still get it down below that into atoms and when you get it into atoms you'll break it up and then what'll you have? Energy. You haven't destroyed matter you've made it change form. There is no way to destroy matter for matter is indestructible. And the substance of matter is mind. Matter is mind appearing. Mind made visible is matter. And to believe otherwise is to believe that which never could be true.

How did this belief come about that matter was an illusion? Only due to the fact, the same fact that wrecked India when it was discovered that the objects of sense are illusion the Indians began to hate their bodies...they refused to save money...they refused to build businesses. What's the use? It's unreal and when we die it'll all disappear. Well you see none of it died and none of it disappeared. They did but not it. The land still is there, the water power still is there, the electricity still is there, the sunshine is there. Every single thing is there that they thought death was going to dissolve.

Gautama the Buddha had the original revelation that is recorded as to the illusory nature of that which we see, hear, taste, touch, and smell. And on the basis of that he did miracle healing works and so did his early disciples. Later on his students or their students misunderstood this word maya or illusion and they thought that the illusion was out here and that this is illusion. No. The concept that we entertain of this is illusion. This isn't. This is so immortal that you can never destroy it. The water can change to steam or it can change to ice but it can't be destroyed and it weighs

53

just as much in any form. This glass, this tumbler can be reduced to splinters. It can be dissolved from our human sight but it cannot be destroyed.
You can take it right back into the laboratory and prove that it has existence and that the existence has weight.

So it is that when metaphysics was first given to the world in the last century the revelation was given that our senses testify erroneously. And instead of staying with that we said, "Oh, no, it isn't our senses it's this that's the illusion." How can an illusion be externalized? How can you get a ghost in your mind to walk this room? How can you get 2 x 2 = 5 to be externalized? How can you get sin, death, and disease to externalize themselves when they exist only in a disordered thought? And all healing is based on that — that sin, disease, and death have no externalized reality. They exist only as externalized illusory beliefs — concepts.

In the first Chapter of Genesis you have an invisible God, an incorporeal God making man and a universe in his own image and likeness. And perhaps you haven't recognized the fact that that man is incorporeal and spiritual and that you've never seen him and never will with your five senses. You never have and you never will. You will never see man with your eyes. You'll never hear him with your ears. You'll never smell him or taste him or touch him. For man is as invisible as God for God and man are one.

Now, what about us? We who see, hear, taste, touch, and smell each other. What about us? Well don't think for a minute that we're unreal. Don't think for a moment that we don't exist. And don't think for a moment that we're an illusion. We aren't. What happened is this — The second chapter of Genesis was written — that was our downfall. Not that it was written — our downfall caused it to be written. In other words a belief was accepted. Don't write me a letter and ask, "How?" I have too many of those.
(laughter) A belief was accepted by us — a belief in two powers — good and evil. And right there and then we lost our heaven, we lost our Eden. And a new world was created. That world has as its essence and substance — mind. Mind which was originally intended to be an avenue of awareness now becomes a creative faculty. And mind forms its own conditions of body. Mind forms its own conditions of form. Mind forms itself, governs itself as matter.

Now here's the proof of it. My mind imbued with Truth is the law of resurrection, renewal, regeneration, restoration to body, to form. My mind imbued with Truth is the mind of those who come to me and of those embraced in my consciousness. My mind imbued with Truth is the mind of individual being. Mind must always form its external appearance. My mind imbued with spiritual truth becomes the instrument through which perfect form appears.

Now watch this in your experience. When you are called upon to heal you have an instrument which is your mind, but before you come into metaphysics your mind is not imbued with spiritual Truth, your mind is ignorant of spiritual Truth. It is an non-illuminated mind. It may be an educated one, but spiritually it's an non-illuminated one. Therefore, if someone says to you, "I have a headache" the best you can do is offer him a pill. But the moment that you are instructed in metaphysical Truth your mind imbued with this Truth becomes a law of healing to that person's headache. And later on when you go far enough to their cancers and consumptions. Mind imbued with Truth — My mind imbued with Truth becomes a law of health to your body, or to your business, or to your home, or to your relationships. Your mind imbued with Truth becomes the law of harmonious form to your family to your patients. Your mind ignorant of Truth results in diseased and discordant bodies. Your mind ignorant of Truth results in poverty, in sin, in false appetites and you can't do anything about it either. Nothing you can do to help yourself. You have to find some medical help of one form or another because your mind has nothing in it of any benefit on this realm of restoration or resurrection. But when you come to Truth, when you come to any of the Truth teachings and your mind becomes imbued with Truth, you are a mental healer. And your mind imbued with Truth becomes the substance of the health of your patient or your student or your friend or your relative.

Now you are functioning in the second chapter of Genesis — a mind created world but not a mind that made a material world there can't be such a thing. The only world a mind can make is a mental world. And therefore, that which we call your physical body while in truth it's a spiritual one to our sense is a mental one because we have formed the concept of body with mind. Our mind fashioned this body and this body was fashioned of mind, therefore its substance is mind and it is mind. And that's why you have the statement "Thoughts are things." Now you can understand that what you hold in your mind as conviction later shows forth in body. Why? Because mind is the substance of body. Mind is the substance of form that we see, hear, taste, touch, or smell, and the way we're seeing it is an illusory picture because that isn't the way it is at all. That's only the way we in our limited sense see it. But it in itself is perfection. Matter is only matter in a material state of consciousness. Once one rises to a mental state it is seen that matter isn't matter at all it is now mind and a process of mind changes the product matter.

16. Specific Principles and Application

You realize now that whatever of the nature of spiritual good — harmony, wholeness — that is to come in to your life, you have to bring in through an activity of your own consciousness. You know now the meaning of "ye shall know the truth and the truth shall make you free", and that you cannot bypass that statement of scripture. It is ye that shall know the truth and ye shall know some very specific truth. There is quite a disagreement at the present time on this subject of freedom of choice, as to whether or not you can know the truth or know more of it than you now know — whether you can be more diligent, more faithful, and more specific.

And according to the Infinite Way it is not possible for you to be other than you are. And if it is your nature to spend 15 or 20 minutes a day with truth there is not much you can do about it, even to increase it for your own good. Even though you know that if you could increase it to two hours a day it would change your whole life. Yet you do not have the capacity to increase that. And for that reason you are doomed to just whatever measure of spiritual good you can assimilate through whatever amount of devotion to truth you are giving. This is unfortunate because there isn't any one of us that would not rejoice if we could be wholly spiritually free. If we could live and move and have our being in God. If we would remain untouched by material law, mental law, the universal beliefs. And yet, until something is awakened in us that compels us to go further and deeper we are victims of inertia.

And the great question is, "Is there any way to overcome this inertia that prevents us from giving ourselves wholeheartedly to the spiritual way of life?" And the answer is, that there is only one way, and that is to recognize that it is inertia that is holding one back. It is inertia that is claiming us, and usually with that recognition we are enabled to break through because up until that moment we do not know what it is that is keeping us back — letting us read one hour a day when we know right well that three or four or five hours would do something to awaken us — or listen to truth for an hour or two instead of idling away that time.

Unless our recognition that it is only inertia that is holding us — unless that recognition changes it for us — we are just going to go along in the mold in which we are going, until something awakens us. And this is sad because it has a sad connotation for the world. It means that because the world, which would love to be free, which would love to be enjoying freedom, which would love to be free of all of the limitations with which we are now surrounded humanly through the new forms of government. While many I'm sure would like to know something of the freedom that was enjoyed in the earlier part of this century, yet this same power of inertia prevents them from doing anything about it. And so it is that we watch our freedom slip away from us — knowing as one professor brought out at a meeting that the people who are trying to prevent the separation of — or rather prevent the amalgamation of church and state, and who think that by fighting this support of schools — parochial schools to be specific — that they are accomplishing that, are really accomplishing nothing, because mathematics is beating them. It will not be long until there is a mathematical supremacy of the Roman Catholic members in the United States.

And that alone will entitle them to the schools and to the government support, and to everything else that they might wish. And inertia alone prevents the right solution, which is by no means a human one. Inertia prevents the Republicans from coming out to the polls, and in England prevents the Conservatives from coming out to the polls — nothing but inertia. There isn't a person who doesn't want what a different form of government would give them, but they don't want it quite enough to go out and vote, even if voting would be the answer, which of course, it isn't.

Do not forget that regardless of what we receive in the balance of this lesson — do not forget that if there is any reason for us not attaining more of what is promised it is because we allow ourselves to be handled by inertia. The promises will be fulfilled in proportion as we can fulfill the terms.

God is individual consciousness. This means that God is your consciousness and mine. God is the consciousness of the individual you and of the individual me. God is the consciousness of all being. Looking at the human scene you would never believe this because it is so impossible to believe that God consciousness can be aware of all of the sins and diseases, lacks, limitations, wars, panics, depressions, which are always on the face of the earth. You have yourself wondered why if there is a God there can be so much of discord in the world, and yet the answer has always been known. In these old religious orders and fraternal orders it has always been known how to bring harmony into individual experience. And here and there in the scriptures of the world we have been told, if we were not told the full truth, we were told near enough to it so that we could have encompassed the balance ourselves. Even when we were told the truth we were not told how to make truth available or tangible in our experience, and this necessarily is an individual experience. And now we are going back to these ancient wisdoms and revealing what these ancients knew that made their lives harmonious, fruitful — even though they did so little for the people of their day regardless of which age we speak of — and, of course, how little we are doing for our generation, and for the same reason — the immediate lack of receptivity and the power of inertia that keeps this world from making the effort necessary.

The very first and most important truth of all is that every bit of good has to come forth from your own consciousness. Those who do not receive this truth always believe that they could pray to a God and under certain circumstances that God would answer the prayer and give the one who prayed that for which they were praying. Of course, there never was a syllable of truth in that entire teaching, regardless of when it was taught, where, or by whom.

And the fact that all of this praying has gone on these thousands of years without being answered must be its own proof. But always this has been truth, that whatever of good is to come forth in the experience of an individual or group or nation, must come forth from the consciousness of an individual.

Now this sets aside the masses from the masters. The masters knew — the masters of the Hebrew world and the masters of the Orient — have always known that it is a matter of "ye shall know the truth and the truth shall make you free". They have always known that whatever is to be brought forth in your experience must come forth from your own consciousness. And, of course, a master is one in whom inertia is not operating to any great extent because they can abide in the Word twenty hours a day, twenty-one, twenty-two, twenty-three, and when necessary twenty-four. And there is no power to prevent it, not even the power of sleep.

Now here is exactly what the situation is — in ordinary human life we are acted upon by universal beliefs — they may be theological beliefs, they may be medical beliefs, they may be scientific beliefs — but they are beliefs, they are not truths. However, these will act in our experience just as if they were the truth until such time as we ourselves know the truth and thereby become free.

Let me explain this for just a moment. The human being awakens in the morning and immediately gets busy about their days activities — dresses, eats, leaves for business, works, shops, is busy all day, returns in the evening, eats, talks, plays, and retires— and all of this while what the Master calls 'this world' is acting upon them. If it is a particularly nasty day there are germs about and he may come home with a cold or a fever. If there is crowded traffic there may be an accident or upset nerves. Or if there is some contagion or infection about, this may occur in his experience. On the other hand, there may be a big business boom, and from this he may prosper. There may be a period of wonderful weather and from this he may benefit. Always whether for good or for evil the world is acting upon the human being. And all the human being can do is wonder whether it will be good today or bad. Whether it will be up or down, rich or poor, healthful or not. The human is not to blame for this. The human has not been taught that it is the activity of our own consciousness that determines the harmony of our own lives.

Now you are being told a wisdom that has been known to the few throughout all ages — that truth maintained in your consciousness — your consciousness maintained active in truth brings forth harmony. In the Master's words "if you abide in the Word and let this Word abide in you, you will bear fruit richly." If you maintain truth active in your consciousness, you are praying without ceasing. And the activity of truth in your consciousness will come forth as harmony, wholeness, completeness, perfection. When you do not entertain this Word, maintain it in your consciousness, then you are "as a branch of a tree that is cut off and withereth."

Therefore, it is you yourself that determines what your life experience is to be. Remember that as a human being you have no such choice. You were never taught this. The power of inertia is at work. At most you were taught that if you were faithful in your church going that God would look graciously upon you, if not in this world then in the next. Or if you obeyed the Ten Commandments.

Well you have lived long enough to know that some of the nicest people in the world haven't had good in this life, and hardly dare expect it in the next.

But the point is — and this is truth — that you can bring a degree of harmony into your experience in every department of life. The degree is always dependent on the degree of your devotion to this work of maintaining truth active in your consciousness. You may accept this as a statement of truth that your mind imbued with truth becomes the law of harmony unto your experience and unto the experience of all those who come within range of your consciousness. Also, a mind not occupied with truth is quickly filled with the beliefs of the world — universal beliefs for which you are not responsible — universal beliefs which were here ages before you appeared on earth and merely plague you because you are on earth, as it will plague all those of the future who are not taught that it is an activity of truth in their own consciousness that maintains the harmony of their lives. One exception to this is that in proportion as we introduce more and more of truth into human consciousness the next generation will be born with less of inertia, with less of world beliefs to overcome.

God functions as individual consciousness when consciousness is imbued with truth.

And what we are going to do and for the rest of this class, we are going to bear witness to this specific truth. We are going to do it in many ways. Let us start with one facet of truth. You will remember that last night we took the first one — God speaking to you says, "Son, thou art ever with me and all that I have is thine." Now this one particular passage must become active in your consciousness for weeks, for months, probably for two or three years, until the world's belief is overcome within you that says first of all that you are separate and apart from God, secondly, that you lack for something.

You see two world beliefs that can forever keep you in poverty.

The first is that you are separate and apart from God, and the second that you can lack. Now just think, "Son, thou art ever with me", is a complete contradiction to the world belief that you have become separated from God and are perhaps trying to find your way back. Or that perhaps some sin of omission or commission has separated you from God and you cannot find your way back. Or that you have not been active in religious or spiritual work and that you have become separated from God. See how many world beliefs operate in your consciousness that eventually convinces you, that you and God are as far apart as the heaven and earth, and how are you ever going to get together. Whereas, the truth reveals that "I and my Father are one", "Son, thou art ever with me", "The place whereon thou standest is holy ground". Just the remembrance of these passages would begin — WOULD within not too long a time if faithfully held to, bring to you again the conscious realization, it is true — where I am, God is, where God is, I am, because from everlasting to everlasting I and my Father ever have been one. I and my Father have been indivisible, inseparable, and the mere fact that I have accepted a world belief of separation, has never separated us.

"I and the Father are one," and this truth need only be realized, maintained in consciousness, until something within gives — human resistance, human disbelief, human doubt gives. And all of a sudden we are interiorly flooded with an assurance, "I have never left Thee", "Before Abraham was, I have been with Thee and I will never leave Thee", "I will be with Thee until the end of the world". And then you realize, how could I have so forgotten scripture. No religious teaching before him ever so completely revealed this to the world or to mankind. He revealed it fully and paid the price. It is being revealed to you again fortunately. We have come so far along in civilization that it is unlikely that any teacher will be persecuted for revealing this truth to you, although they may be misunderstood and slandered. But it is up to you in that event to know whether or not you have been told the truth — demonstrable truth — truth to which you can bear witness in your experience.

Do you see that by neglecting these passages of scripture and leaving them out of your mind that you have left your mind open to all of the suggestions that the world can pour in? Whereas, if you maintain this truth, if you abide in this truth, if you dwell in this truth, live and move and have your being in the truth that "I and the Father are one", and that this is an everlasting relationship, so that the place whereon I stand is holy ground, and there are no human laws or human beliefs of a physical or mental nature that can separate me from the love of God, or the Presence of God, or the Power of God, and then maintain this in the face of all appearances to the contrary.

The way is straight and narrow and still there be few that enter because this truth must be held to in spite of appearances to the contrary. When the storm was rising at sea the prophet had to look right at the disciples and wonder at their lack of faith. When there seemed to be multitudes to be fed and no food, he must have wondered at his disciples. In every illustration of healing it must have been clear that he was revealing that right where you are God is — "What did hinder you? Pick up your bed and walk."

As you maintain this truth you will go on to the next. "Son, thou art ever with me and all that I have is thine." Well now, here is the answer to lack and limitation of any nature, every nature — physical, mental, moral, financial — this is the answer. "All that I have is thine." Where is this "I" that has this all-ness that is mine? It is closer to you than breathing and nearer than hands and feet. And every time that you say "I", that is the "I" that has this all-ness that is yours for the accepting.

Every time you realize "I" will never forsake me, "I" will never leave me, "I" will be with me until the end of the world, you are declaring that here where "I" am God is. Because "I and the Father are one", this is the reason that all that "I" the Father hath belongs to "I" the Son. Because they are not two. And there are not two places, and the Father does not have to send you your good. In fact He couldn't. It is already closer to you than breathing and nearer than hands and feet. And we must open out a way for the imprisoned splendor to escape. We must acknowledge that "I and the Father are one", that the Father has never left me, that the Father will never leave me, because of Oneness. I am your bread, and I am your wine, and I am your water.

You can never be separated from food, or clothing, or housing, or companionship, or infinite good as long as your consciousness is active in maintaining this truth. Separate yourself from truth and you have separated yourself from me — from the I within your being, for I am the truth. Separate yourself from truth and you have separated yourself from what? From life. From supply. For truth and love and life and supply, intelligence, wisdom, bread, wine, water, meat, resurrection — these are all synonyms, one for another. In separating yourself from truth you are separating yourself from the good. The good of God's kingdom manifest on this plane. But as you maintain truth in your consciousness, you maintain life, love, peace, supply, companionship, wisdom, guidance, direction, protection, infinity itself — but it all depends on your consciously abiding in truth and letting truth abide in you.

17. Treatment and Law to Grace

And so it was that my life became a dedication to meditation so that I might learn the laws. I couldn't learn them externally because I hadn't been able to find them anywhere. And so I had to go within to see if it could be revealed to me what it was that brought these experiences. And, of course, the result of these meditations, the result of these many, many spiritual experiences some of which have lasted for a period of two whole months, some three days, some one day, some five days, these are embodied in my writings.

The first and most important one deals with the origin of evil, the nature of evil and how to deal with it. And strangely enough this contradicts every metaphysical teaching which is on the face of the earth today. This is a direct contradiction of the principles that are ordinarily taught because it says this — "All evil regardless of its name or nature is impersonal." And that means that it is not your wrong thinking that has caused your troubles. And it is not your envy or jealous or malice. It is not your sensuality. It is not your lack of gratitude. It is not your anything. There isn't a single thing in you that is responsible for any of your ills. And the very moment that you seek within yourself or within your patients for the cause of the trouble you are helping to perpetuate it. And you're making it almost impossible to be healed. And when you do heal it's more or less accidentally or because you have caught some absolute statement of truth which has made you rise higher than your own beliefs. In other words, if you are a thief don't condemn yourself it is not your fault and it is not your nature. And if you are too sensual don't try to correct yourself and to be the opposite of that whatever the opposite may be. If you are envious or jealous or malicious don't try to stop it and don't try to make it something else because if you succeed you will just still be a human being with a little different qualities than you had before — probably a little better but you'll still be a human being. In other words, you'll just be a person who has "psychologized" themselves into suppressing that which is within them until sometime it breaks out like Spring. The evil that is finding expression in you, the error, whether it is finding expression as a disease, as a false trait, as an evil character, as a false appetite has absolutely nothing to do with you, it didn't begin in you, and you'll never root it out of you. You never will.

It was the reason that Dr. Menninger was able to say on a nationwide broadcast that in his experience in psychology not a single cure of anything has ever been achieved. Of course, we believe we're on the right track but in 75 years we haven't proven it in a single case. Why? Because the basis of it is that the error is within you and we'll find it and correct it. But they haven't found it in you and if they did they couldn't correct it.

Now then, evil has its origin in something that we may for this moment term the carnal mind. If the carnal mind means nothing to you, you can call it Satan. And if

Satan is too far back in your religious life to have any meaning you can call it mortal mind. If you don't like Satan, carnal mind, or mortal mind, you can call it an appearance, a claim, or an illusion. The name you give it is unimportant. The important thing is to know that it is a universal impersonal source of any and every form of evil. Unless you can do that — in other words, unless you can see a man stealing a pocketbook and then say, "Thank God I know you aren't the thief.
The carnal mind is behind this, or mortal mind, or a claim." Unless you can separate that evil from that individual you haven't a ghost of a show of healing him. If you are confronted with a case of cancer and you are tempted to believe that jealousy, hatred, sensuality caused it, you haven't a chance to be a good healer even if accidentally you do heal someone once in a while because none of those things cause cancer. Cancers have been caused in newborn babies and they haven't had a chance yet to be hateful or sensual or anything else. And there are some mighty fine pure men and women in the world who have these diseases who never knew such things as hate or sensuality or jealousy to the extent of causing a cancer.

Unless you can instantly impersonalize by realizing that this claim has its origin in an impersonal source whether you call it carnal mind or mortal mind makes no difference. But don't have it in your patient. Don't have it in your student. And above all things don't have it in yourself. And right here I'm going to tell you why. You might as well know it at the beginning because I know you're all students of many years standing. The reason is God constitutes your identity, your name is I. And you know it, you call yourself I. That's the only way you can identify yourself is as I. And that I is your identity but that I is God, and how dare you say that it has evil qualities and propensities. I have no evil qualities or propensities.

And so it is that you and I might say that there is time when we feel sensual. Maybe there is even times when we feel envious. But don't start condemning yourself. That is just a universal thing that you picked up out of the ether and it has no relationship to you because the minute you know that I am I — "I and my Father are one and all that the Father hath is mine." — you'll know that you have no evil qualities, no evil propensities, and no evil characteristics and that any that are within you they are but the projection of that which we will call carnal mind or mortal mind or Satan — meaning impersonal source of evil. Now when you have done this you have got your patient about half cured. As long as you lift the burden of guilt you have them just about half cured and you can complete it with the next step although for believers the next step is going to be a bitter pill to swallow.

In the next step you'll have to agree that the Bible made a terrible mistake. That the Bible made a mistake that has helped to keep us in bondage. The Bible made a mistake that has been fatal to the world. The Bible said, "The carnal mind is enmity against God." And don't you believe it. The carnal mind is a belief in two powers. Anywhere that the belief in two powers exists you have a carnal mind.

63

18. Contemplation Develops the Beholder

Many times we — especially the younger student — is opt to believe that the spiritual way of life, the contemplative way of life is one without discipline, and the very opposite of this is true because there is no life that requires more discipline than the spiritual life.

The human life as much as we think that it is disciplined is more or less an undisciplined one because no attempt is made to control, or little attempt is made to control the nature of our thinking. We are more apt to accept everything that we see or hear and then rejoice over what we think is good and start to moan over what we believe to be evil. So that we don't really discipline ourselves to ask "Is this as good as it appears to be?" or "Is this as evil as it appears to be?" But rather we accept appearances in accordance with our own judgments. And in the spiritual way of life that cannot be done. As a matter of fact the entire spiritual way life is built on the rejection of appearances.

In the metaphysical life such as you have in Religious Science and Unity, New Thought — you always have the rejection of an appearance of evil — the denial of an appearance of evil. The realization of the unreal nature of all that is appearing as evil — as error. But when you get to the spiritual life you have to go beyond that because you have to deny reality to that which appears good. You have to un-see the humanly good to the same extent that you have to un-see the humanly evil. And the reason is that spiritually discerned there is neither good nor evil and the entire spiritual universe is built on that.

"Why callest thou me good?" or "Neither do I condemn thee."

In other words, I am not sitting in judgment on what appears to be evil but neither am I accepting the appearance of good. Why? Because the only real is the invisible spiritual and that can't be seen with the eyes and it can't be heard with the ears. And therefore, the discipline on this path lies in rejecting every appearance whether it is good or evil in the realization that whatever it is that is of God is invisible to the human senses.

Now the effect of that when it is successfully accomplished is this: If I am confronted with an appearance out here and I judge it to be evil I immediately have to resist evil or overcome evil or destroy it or remove it. If on the other hand I am confronted with an appearance out here of human good I am forced to accept it and rejoice in it. And the danger of that is that the very thing that appears to me good may in and of itself be evil, or may change to evil, or its effect upon one may be evil. The commonest illustration of that is that everybody would agree that a million dollars is good, or getting a million dollars is good, and yet getting a million dollars has ruined more people than it has helped. It has changed their nature. It has made them grasping. Even people who have little or nothing and who ordinarily are free and joyous in sharing it — the very moment that they have a little begin to start hording it and grasping it and laying it up for a rainy day and fearing to spend it. So that what would appear to be good has for them turned into an evil.

And so it is in the human picture, everyone without exception rejoices at a birth, and everyone without exception sorrows at a death. And certainly more trouble is caused in the world by birth than ever was caused by death. And so, if you are going to judge from human appearances think of the tragedies that take place with all of this rejoicing at birth and think of the nonsense of much of the sorrowing at death. Because strangely enough there is just as much sorrowing when a person goes on in far advanced years and has outlived their usefulness to themselves or to anyone else on Earth and yet the sorrowing goes on. As if something were being lost or something were being hurt. Now, these are but extreme illustrations of the fact that it is unwise to judge of good or evil, but spiritually it goes beyond being unwise. In a spiritual sense it becomes absolutely a wrong thing and for this reason. There is a power that is within each and every one of us, and this power has as its function the creating, maintaining, and sustaining of harmony in our existence, or when for any reason harmony is taken from our lives its function is to restore it.

Now, how can I bear witness except by being still? If I do anything other than be still, I can no longer say that I am doing nothing and that I am nothing. I have become something the moment I do something. Therefore, when I am confronted with appearances — now it makes no difference whether human-hood calls the appearance good or human-hood calls the appearance evil. I am confronted with a human appearance and if I would bear witness to the presence of God I must do nothing, I must think nothing and I must have no judgment. I must immediately, in order to make myself nothing, I must realize within myself there is neither good nor evil there is but God. And now as I look out at the erroneous appearance with no judgment — there is neither good nor evil, there is only the presence of God, and then I'm still. And now the Father within me can perform Its function and Its function then is to destroy the appearance and reveal God's glory — His own being. So that, even though to our sense a healing appears, it isn't really a healing it is the destruction of the material picture and the making visible of the spiritual one. But there is only one way in which we can do that and that way is to have no judgment as to good or evil in the appearance and then let the Father within me do the work. Then and then only can we say, "I had nothing to do with this demonstration except to bear witness to God in action."

19. The Healing Principles

(Special Lesson on Healing Work)

Those who have not spent considerable time practicing these principles will for a while forget and thereby delay the experience of good. And this is what they will forget. We do not look to each other for anything. And that means husbands and wives, parents and children. The very earliest that we can in the morning we open ourselves to God's Grace and consciously realize, that we live not by might nor by power but by the Spirit. We live not by bread alone but by every word that proceedeth out of the mouth of God.

Nor do we live by the favor of individuals or the goodwill of individuals. Nor do we live by our place or position in life. We live by the Grace of God. Now if we are to live in the mystical consciousness we must abide in this that our expectancy is always and only from the Spiritual source that is within us. The Spiritual life, the Spiritual spring, the Spiritual bread, meat, wine, water. We must abide in this truth that "I have meat the world knows not of" and then be careful that we are not looking to a person, a thing, an organization, a relationship for it. Now when we are thoroughly understood this Oneness, thoroughly realized as if I were the only person in the world, and yet my good must flow, because it must flow from within me, not to me from anyone, but from me through me. When I have done that it makes no difference that my good will come in through people. It may come through you, it may come through other students, it may come through but it doesn't have to. There is no law that says so. There is no law that says, "I must derive my income from my work." No law, no rule says so.

Because within me must be the complete realization that my manna can fall from the sky if it's necessary. Ravens can bring my food. My supply can come from a thousand different directions. Therefore, I need not look to anyone, yet of course, there must always be that sense of gratitude to those through whom it comes. But not the feeling that it comes from them. It comes through them, it comes from the center of my being because remember the word is "I", and "I" is infinite, and there is nothing and no one outside of me. Therefore, all that is to be mine must flow from the "I" of my being. Then when I do that I can be as free as I wish to be in sharing. And just as free in receiving — grateful for the opportunity to share, grateful for receiving, but never for a moment moving to left or right from my inner conviction that I and my Father are one. And my good is derived from that relationship. The relationship of "I and my Father are one" is the source of my good. So with you. And, the importance of this is that when you demonstrate it, you are in the position of demonstrating it for those who come to you.

What are the problems of those that come to you? You will discover you could boil it down to personal sense, but personal sense means that there are two or more people.

There can be man and wife. There can be parent and child. There can be partners in business. There can be capital and labor relations. There can be all kinds of human relationships and every one of them at some time or other is the source of discord and disharmony. And if you are called upon for help you have only one remedy to give spiritually and that is your realization of "I". "I and my Father are one" and in that relationship is infinite relationship — the only relationship there is and so we don't have me and a God. And we don't have me and a partner. And we don't have me and another person at the conference table. We only have the "I" that I am infinitely expressed. Then when we sit down at the conference table, a unity unfolds, a oneness of thought unfolds, a mutual-ness unfolds. It does so not because anyone has "psychologized" it but because someone has realized there are not two at the conference table there is but one and I am that one. "I" God, am that one. "I" constitute me and "I" constitute you. "I" God constitutes individual being and until you reduce the relationships of everyone to one you are still dealing with a human world and trying to patch it up. Now you can succeed temporarily just as we have had the end of wars temporarily and then the start of other wars. But for permanent peace to be established in your household, in your community, in your business, in your profession, there is only one way. Don't have a patient, a practitioner and a God. Come to the realization that "I" am the only one. And when you are abiding in that I-ness, the infinite individuality appearing as two or more people will be one. One in purpose, one in solution of problems, and one in will.

Now this embodies for a while a discipline, a training — because every time we look out here humanly we see two or more. And what do we find? This one has a will in this way, and this one has a will in that way, someone else has another will, and you sit three people down together each with a will of their own and you've got a war. But the solution to it from your standpoint as a practitioner is not to have three people to the deal or thirty three. Resolve them into one by realizing there is only one life, there is only one mind, there is only one law, there is only one Spirit, there is only one will. And "I am" is that one. So whether "I am" is Joel, "I am" is Bill, "I am" is Mary, it is still "I am", it is still the one that "I am", and I am that "I am". Then you see you have resolved this thing to where you don't have patient, practitioner, and God — nor do you have three people or thirty three people each with a will of their own. In a Spiritual activity you do not bring two together to make them one. You realize there was only one to begin with and "I am" that one. The "I" of me is that one. Then, you can say, "Thy will be done." "Thy will be done," meaning that "I" which is the "I" of each of us. And when thy will is done it is made manifest in all who are concerned.

In this work health is only one of the problems that comes to us, and a great deal of the health problems are caused by personal relationship problems. Unhappiness in the home, unhappiness in business. And this works on the system eventually to bringing ill health. So try to see that every problem that is brought to you for solution involves reducing the appearance to one. And that one — "I". In your own individual experience when you are dealing with people and can realize there is only one will — only one will — and the "I" of me is that will or the "I" of you. There is only one will. There is only one desire. There is only one interest. Within the "I" that I am there cannot be conflicting interests so there's no use of trying to reconcile them. Do not try to reconcile interests because this is psychology. This is a human patching up of the scene. There is no conflicts of interest because "I am" one. And in that oneness there can be no conflict.

The more you ponder in your meditation the great Truth of Within-ness, the closer you come to living the Spiritual life. The more you are able to perceive that it is He that is within me that doeth the works, or it is He that is within me that performs — or perfects. It is He that is within me that guides, leads, directs. And then realize of course, it isn't a he because that would mean he and me. The he that were speaking of is the "I" that I am. The Selfhood — the one infinite divine Selfhood that I am and you are. You begin to live from a different standpoint. Not the standpoint of getting, achieving, accomplishing, but the standpoint of being and sharing. Being! Nothing to come from without — all to flow from within.

20. The Attitude and Altitude of Prayer

We are uniting consciously with our source which is God. Remember we are already one with God. That is a relationship that never can be broken. I and my Father are one. This is an eternal relationship which began before Abraham was in the beginning and it will continue until the end of time. But the prodigal experience in which we left our Father's house — in other words we broke our contact with divine consciousness, at least in our mind, in our belief, has set us up as separate and apart from God.

Now remember we could not be separate and apart from God in reality, it is only as a dream experience or an illusory experience of the mind just like you could close your eyes now and decide that you will leave this room, and without leaving your seat you would in time if you persisted in that — you would cut yourself off from what is being said and revealed here, and insofar as you are concerned it would be the same as if you had left the room. In other words, you broke the mental contact or spiritual contact and you might continue hearing the words in your ear and yet they make no impression in your consciousness. Why? You have mentally broken the contact.

So it was that as prodigals we never did leave our Father's house because the Father won't release us. As a matter of fact the Father couldn't release us because I and the Father are one. He'd have to break Himself in two in order to get rid of us and you can't break infinity at any point or it would no longer be infinity. Now, since I and the Father are one, the only way that I can lose my inheritance is by mentally cutting myself off and saying, "I'm no longer one with my Father. I'm going to be something of myself." And then I've really created a selfhood apart from God but I've only done it in the mind, I haven't done it in Truth. And at any moment I can awaken, and just by an activity of consciousness, return to my Father's house, the house I never left. So watch this in your meditation now — you are agreeing that I and the Father are one and that the kingdom of God is within me. And so now I am not returning to my Father's house but I am becoming conscious of the fact that I never left my Father's house — that I and my Father are one, always have been one, always will be one, for I will never leave thee nor forsake thee. Then what happens when we are consciously one with God — go back to the example of the tree now, and you'll find that you are also one with every other branch that is on that tree. In other words, you are now one with companionship, with supply, with home, with activity, with fruitfulness — you are one with every branch on God's tree. All because you are one with the Father. You are one with every child of God.

When you enter meditation in this light you are fulfilling what I brought out last night about the attitude and the altitude of prayer. The attitude of prayer or meditation is, "I am returning to my Father's house. I am going within to commune with the Spirit within me. I am recognizing, "I and the Father are one." I am the branch reuniting with the tree — becoming consciously aware as one with the tree. I am becoming conscious of my oneness with God, and in my oneness with all Spiritual being, idea — with life, with love, with substance, with law, with peace, joy, dominion — ah, yes, above all — in my oneness with God, I am one with the grace of God. In my oneness with God I receive God's grace. In my oneness with God I receive the benediction of God. The Spirit of the Lord God is upon me when I am in communion with my Father within. The Spirit of the Lord God is upon me. His Spirit dwells in me and this, ah, this — "If so be the Spirit of God dwelleth in you, then are you the child of God, and if a child heir, joint heir with all mankind to all the heavenly riches, if so be the Spirit of God dwell in you."

And I am in meditation now for only one reason — that I may be consciously aware that the Spirit of God dwells in me — that His Spirit is upon me, that His grace is with me, that His benediction touches me. I am here in prayer, in meditation — not to ask for anything, not to demand anything, not even to desire anything — only to know that I in the midst of me is God. Only to know that I can do all things through this indwelling Spirit, the image of God in me. I am only here in meditation for one purpose to know that I live, yet not I, this Spirit of God in me, this indwelling Spirit is living my life — that this indwelling Spirit is my bread, and my meat, and my wine, and my water — is the resurrection unto my whole experience. Even the lost years of the locust are restored to me by this indwelling Spirit. Thy grace is my sufficiency in all things. In this meditation I am realizing that thy grace is with me, and it is my sufficiency. I need not ask for anything for thou knowest my need even before I do. I need not ask for anything for it is thy good pleasure to give me the kingdom. My part is to dwell humbly in the house of the Lord. My part is to acknowledge that "except the Lord build the house, they labor in vain that build it." In meditation I acknowledge Him in all my ways. I acknowledge that God is my life, the very substance of my body, the law unto my existence. I acknowledge that I live by God's grace — not by might, not by power, but by God's grace — by this Spirit of God indwelling.

This is the attitude of prayer — the attitude, acknowledgement, recognition, realization. This is the attitude and the motive. And, the altitude is when having voiced this or thought this, I'm silent. "Speak Lord thy servant heareth." And then wait for that Spirit to consciously be upon me — for that Spirit to announce Itself and say, "Fear not, I am with thee. I will never leave thee. I will be with thee unto the end of the world. I am thy meat, thy wine, thy water. I am the resurrection unto thy whole experience. I in the midst of you am mighty." This is the altitude when the still small voice speaks to us — when we have finished speaking within and when the voice begins to speak to us — not necessarily audibly, and yet leaving us with this impression, "I have been touched by the Spirit. I have received thy grace, thy benediction." And there you have the attitude of prayer and you have the altitude of prayer this is the same in meditation.

70

21. Attaining "That Mind"

When Dr. Steinmetz said that the nature of spiritual power would be revealed in the 20th Century it should have shaken the foundations of the entire religious world. Because nothing would be more natural than to assume that the religions of the world knew all about spiritual power because supposedly religions are based on spiritual power. And yet no one seems to have been shocked by that statement and so far as I know no one has made the claim that the nature of spiritual power was well known.

Actually, the reason that the nature of spiritual power has not been known is this — that spiritual power does not belong to the mind — to the intellect. There is no amount of knowledge that anyone can attain that would be spiritual power. There is no amount of knowledge that anyone could attain that would move mountains spiritually or heal disease spiritually or raise the dead or forgive the sinner. You cannot forgive the sinner by saying, "I forgive you." You cannot heal the sick by pleading with God to heal the sick. You cannot multiply loaves and fishes spiritually by any means now known to the human mind.

It is because of this that we know that spiritual power can only be brought into expression through the attainment of a fourth dimensional consciousness — a higher awareness than that which is possessed by the human mind. In other words, there is no known truth that will ever function spiritually. It makes no difference what truth you study or what truth you believe you know. Whether it is one of the more orthodox appeals to God or whether it is using the words of the Bible, "I say unto thee pick up thy bed and walk." or "I say unto thee arise." or "Thou seest me thou seest the Father that sent me." Use these statements, memorize these truths, and do anything you like with them and you will find that there is no spiritual power in them. Take any of the statements that have ever been given to the world by any of the modern metaphysical teachings — learn them by heart — if you like learn them even forwards and backwards, and see if they will result in any spiritual activity and you will find that the answer is 'no'. You will find that there are students who have studied 10, 20, 30, 40 years and still haven't achieved the healing of a headache, and yet they know all of the words in the Bible and they know all of the words in the metaphysical books. In the same way there are great biblical scholars — very few of them have ever attempted to perform anything of a spiritual nature with all of the knowledge they possess. And the reason is it isn't possible. It isn't possible to bring the least spiritual power into expression by any means now known to the intellect or to the mind and yet any person with even a grain of spiritual attainment can do mighty works that the greatest minds could never perform. That is why the Master said that you must come as little children, not as great scholars, not as men and women who know a great deal about scripture or truth but as a little child.

It is for this reason that our work is quite a difficult one. It is the only work of its kind anywhere in the Western world where the entire goal of our work is the attaining of some measure of spiritual consciousness. Our work is not the imparting of knowledge because all of the knowledge, all of the letter of truth that there is in the message of the Infinite Way can be imparted in any one week in the year. It would require only one week of anyone's time to learn all of the letter of truth — to learn all that we know — all that's embodied in our books. Every bit of this could be learned in one week as far as the mind, the intellect is concerned. What good it would do I don't know except if an individual decided to take that knowledge and work with it and practice it until it served its purpose in developing the higher consciousness.

In the Orient this is quite a different story. This manner of teaching has been known in the Orient since long, long centuries before the Common era. It is that system whereby there is a spiritual teacher that is one who has attained some measure (some have more and some less) of spiritual consciousness, and by sitting quietly in their cave or in their mountain place or by the river bank, gradually attract to themselves some individuals who feel drawn to them or led to them, and then these become the student body and they will sit around with the teacher, come back each day for a session, sometimes remain for two or three or four nights and days, sleeping outdoors if necessary until some measure of light begins to dawn in their consciousness. Other teachers have graduated from their caves and formed ashrams — small houses, temples, places of worship and living, and students come to them — drawn there because there is no advertising, and you have the same thing repeated. People sometimes come from thousands of miles away just to spend a week or two with a particular teacher. Usually the local students will come and remain anywhere up to five, six, seven years because in the Orient, in spite of radio and television, they still don't know that we think you can learn spiritual truth over a busy weekend. And so they feel that it's quite normal and natural to spend three, four, five, six, seven years with their teacher.

However, the teacher is never imparting very much of truth because the teacher knows very little of truth, and in fact there isn't much really of truth to impart. And so it becomes a matter of meditation — of imparting a truth here and there with which the student can work, meditate, and ponder, until they attain some degree of awareness of even one particular truth.

In the experience of some of these students they reach a place that the teacher recognizes where they are ready not to live now as the disciples said, "We can do all things in thy name." In other words, through your consciousness. But where they are now ready to live on their own consciousness, and usually the Oriental teacher sends the student out away from him for a year or two until the student proves that they have been able to live on their own consciousness — their own degree of attainment, and then usually they receive their title, their robe, and they in turn go out and either sit in a cave or start a small ashram, or in these modern days travel to the Western world and start teaching.

All of this is aimed at one thing — the development of a higher consciousness than the normal intellect or human mind — the development of a state of consciousness which is not normal to the human being because it has never been developed in the human being although it is there. In the beginning, before what is called Adam and Eve, every individual had a fully developed spiritual consciousness — in fact, that's all they did have — they didn't have what we call mortal consciousness because they had no awareness of good and evil. They had no more awareness of good than they did of evil. They only had an awareness of being — harmonious being, joyous being, free being. There was neither Greek nor Jew. There was neither bond nor free. There was only being. Pure being. And each individual drew their wisdom, their substance, their support, their life from the Source which was the Divine Consciousness called the Father Consciousness. The Father Consciousness is this Supreme Consciousness. The Son Consciousness is the full and complete individualization of the Father Consciousness.

In other words, when an individual drew entirely from their spiritual source they had that same mind that the Father had and they had the fullness of it without in any wise taking away any that their neighbor had. Just as your garden can have the full sunshine without depriving your neighbor's garden of any sunshine. It too can have the full sunshine.

Now, after what is called the fall of man. After what is called the departure from the Garden of Eden, the expulsion from the Garden of Eden, man has a consciousness of his own. He no longer has the Father's consciousness, he now has a mortal consciousness, that is the suffix 'al' meaning 'of' a consciousness of death. As everyone has who is under the universal belief in two powers. That very belief in two powers means life and death, good and evil, rich and poor, pure and sinful. That is the dual consciousness of the human race, the mortal consciousness, the consciousness of death. Now, ever since the beginning of religion the attempt has been to get back into the Garden of Eden, or in the language of the prodigal son who also was the son of the king, the son of nobility, royalty, kingliness, and wealth, and as a son was heir to all his father had, but he too entertained a sense of separation and decided to be an individual on his own account with no dependence on his source, no dependence on the Father, but rather, "I me of my own self am mighty." And so he departs with whatever measure of his father's substance his father gave him — and remember it was divided — and then every bit that he used left him with a little bit less until he ran out of consciousness, ran out of substance, and had nothing left not even to eat. And from the moment that he turned in recognition of this fact, turned back to the father's house he also exemplified the place that we exist now in the human scale where we realize we have come to the end of our rope. We have used up all of our resources. We have no way of knowing how to maintain peace

73

on earth — certainly, no way of knowing how to prolong life and we're ready to acknowledge — those that are in the Father's house, even if they're servants there, are a lot better off than we are facing tomorrow's headlines.

22. God Made This World For Men and Women

If you are mind readers you'd all be laughing now. If you'd have read my mind it would have really been a vaudeville show for you because I was sitting here and I was thinking of the most tragic thing in the world that I could possibly think about. And you know what it was, it was a little chicken just before it bites its way out of the egg. I was thinking of this little chick, locked up inside of the egg — the full and complete chicken. And I was trying to live its feelings, wondering a little bit really what it had to live for. If it looked around inside there it was pretty dark. It might even feel a sense of hunger and there was no food there. And above all things there was no companionship. Here's this lone little chick locked up — tightly locked up in this egg. It had nothing to be happy about but on the other hand it had nothing to be unhappy about because it didn't know what it was missing. It hadn't ever known the world.

All it knew was being locked up in there and not even knowing that it was locked up inside of this egg shell. Now as far as the chick is concerned, I could see that that chick in and of itself might stay there forever, just living in that darkness or living as long as it didn't starve. It might even find enough food in there to keep it alive — not much more than that — keep it existing. It wouldn't really be living it would be existing in there and of itself it could do nothing about it. There it is and there it's doomed to be. But fortunately, fortunately for these little chicks there is something beyond themselves. There is something that causes that chick to peck at the shell and to keep pecking at it until it breaks a hole in it — until it sees some light. Oh, I suppose we could think of what goes on in a little chick's thought when it begins to catch that light outside and realize, "Uh, oh, there's something out there. Something I haven't seen, something I haven't felt, maybe some place I haven't been." And it keeps pecking away, it keeps pecking away. . .

Something is making it do this. We'll call it a force of nature like the unborn child just before it's born that is being urged forward, forward, out, out. Not of its own self, it knows nothing about an outside world, it has no desire to get out. Probably left to itself it thinks, "I'm pretty warm and comfortable here." But there is something urging. We call it a force of nature that eventually would compel that child to be born. Something would compel that chick to break that shell and come outside and find a great big world — a tremendous big yard to go looking for food, and oh, the amount of food in that yard, and all the other chicks out there to play with, and some rain. You know more than I do, I've never been on a farm, but you know what things that chicks going to find in the first six hours that it's out of its shell — more things than a child is going to find in a toy store.

And here it is now, no longer restricted, no longer bound, but with the ability to look out there and see a million things, and hear things, and feel things, and experience things in a great big world. And what made me think of all this was the fact that going around and around inside here has been a thought that men, women, and children are prisoners of the mind. Think of the average man, woman, and child, and see if they aren't locked up inside of their mind, and they know not what is going on in this world except what's going on in here — what they're thinking, their own limitations. They are living in there restricted — restricted — limited. They don't know about the free world. They don't know about the coal in the ground, the oil in the ground, the diamonds, the platinum, the gold and silver and copper, pearls in the sea.

They don't know anything. All they're doing is living inside here — in a shell that we call the skull. And that's where the average person is living inside of their skull. Seeing only their own thoughts. Believing only their own concepts — their own limitations. It's a terrible world to live in, the world of one's mind because that mind doesn't know anything beyond its own limitations. It knows nothing except what its experienced, or what its parents told it, or its Sunday school teacher, or somebody else that may have had a limited concept of the world. And so it accepts every kind of belief that's given to it. It accepts every kind of law of limitation. It finally settles down on a little plot of ground about 20' by 60' and calls it home — lucky if they ever get one that's 100' by 100', or calls that home. They eat, they drink, they sleep, they have families, but they are on a treadmill. They are living a life of limitation locked up in here, not knowing a think about the great big world and the wonderful people in the world. [They] know nothing about the cattle on a thousand hills, the great mountains and the great seas, and even if they see them around they just see them as scenery.

Some few are fortunate that the law, whether we want to call it nature or whether we want to call it God — something stirs inside of the mind and makes them wonder, "Is there something beyond this that I know? Is there something beyond this that I'm seeing with my eyes, or hearing with my ears, or thinking with my mind?" We call it a desire to know God or we call it a desire for Truth or a reaching out for Truth. Sometimes it comes in the form of ambition that makes a person want to break through their present circumstances and get out into a wider atmosphere of life — a broader atmosphere — something beyond their present limitations. Because remember this, there are no limitations.

Just for a moment take the blinkers off your own eyes and think of this ocean out front here, and the mountains around, and the world beyond the mountains, and the world beyond the seas, and notice. Well it might be a moonlight night — notice the moon up there and it's shining on the ocean — beauty. The pictures it presents to us of a vast infinity. Not only up in the sky but all around us in the sea or lighting up those mountains, showing us something so vast, so far beyond our immediate reach. Or looking away from the moon into the dark part of the sky and see those millions of stars each one a world, each one containing a story, each one containing an experience, each one telling us some kind of a story of its light, of its fire, of its being, of its reason for being right where it is, of that which caused it to be.

Come down again to the daytime. Let's travel a few miles around the island and see the vastness of space even on a small island — the cattle on a thousand hills, trees, plants. And then begin to ask yourself why they are there. What they're doing there? What purpose do they serve? And what do you think the answer would be if you could view all of this and then say to yourself, "Supposing there were no men or women on earth, to what purpose would all of this be? To what purpose would all of this be? To what purpose would it be that there is a sun, a moon, stars — that there's cattle on a thousand hills — that there's tremendous trees of all kinds, plants, flowers, blooms, vegetables, fruits, diamonds in the ground, pearls in the sea? To what purpose if there isn't a man, if there isn't a woman, if there isn't what we know as human life on earth — which isn't human life at all because once you begin to peck your way through this shell of the human mind and look outside — you'll find that all of this is there for you and me. The earth is the Lord's and the fullness thereof, and Son, all that I have is Thine. Everything that exists, exists for you and for me. God has created a tremendous universe. But why? Why? Not only for birds to fly around in and fish to swim around in but that we should travel around in and own this — enjoy this. And I don't mean own it in the sense of having title to a little piece of land because it is only when you travel up in these modern planes, 10, 20, 30, 40 thousand feet and look down — even if you do say to yourself, "I own a mile of that?" you're a pretty puny individual if you think in terms of owning. But when you can look down on there and say, "I'm a man...a woman. I'm a creature of God, and God made this for me — for my enjoyment."

I wonder how these people feel who pay a million or two million dollars for a painting, and know that we are going to have the pleasure of looking at as much as they are for just a ten cent admission. I think it must make them feel kind of foolish — the sense of possession. How can you possess these works of art?

Nobody possesses them except those who enjoy them. Those who enjoy them have the true sense of possession. So it is with the land and so it is with the sea. Nobody can buy an ocean and nobody can really buy a large enough piece of land to call it so. And yet, if only we lift the restriction of this mind — come out of this iron clad skull and instead of seeing our own limited thoughts, our own man-made limitations — mind-made limitations — come out of it and live — not exist anymore by eating three meals a day or having a place to sleep or a family to be with but come out. Come out of that mind and live and begin to see that a universe such as we have here must have been created by nothing less than what we call God. To have created this universe takes all the wisdom of an infinite intelligence, of a divine love, a great love. But love for what or whom? It must have been a love for us that all of this is given to us to love, to enjoy.

Oh you could go back to the art works that have come down to us for generations and generations, even as we have seen it over in Egypt, and in the Holy Lands, or in the Near East, or the Far East, these great treasures that have come down from thousands of years and they're here for us. The people who created them didn't own them. And the proof of it is, they had to give them up and they had to give them up to all of the rest of the world who came afterward. And that's why they're here — not for us to own, to possess, but for us to own and enjoy through this knowledge that there must be a God.

There is a God. There is something — a Spirit that has created this great universe and then set us down in it.

And here it is:

You see if we keep compressing ourselves inside of this skull, we're going to have no more vision than the chicken that's inside of that shell. That's going to be the limit of its world and this skull is going to be the limit of our world. And the little thoughts we think — we think, because they are the thoughts that come from just looking around the room we're in or the town we're in.

We haven't opened our mind to receive the pictures from the Universal Mind. To receive the awareness of the divine qualities that exist throughout this world — the divine qualities that constitute art and literature and science — the qualities that exist as the love of men and women. I don't only mean the family love, I'm talking about the love of relationships on a world wide scale, on an impersonal and personal scale, but yet a love that is not limited to just a few people that are around us — a sharing in the love of people throughout the world. How can we be aware of the fact that there are people anywhere in the world? There's only one way, you have to peck that shell open. You have to break through the limitations of this mind that tries to tell you there are only the people around us — the territory around us. And we have to open our vision until the first thing you know, we are aware of sun, moon, and stars. We are aware of oceans and of mountains, and the first thing you know our vision goes wider and wider and wider, and the first thing you know like Christopher Columbus we're looking across the sea. And the first thing you know we're discovering that there's land across the sea. We haven't seen it with our eyes but now we've stopped this limited thinking based on only what we know and we've opened ourselves to what God knows. The God that placed us here and that placed all of this here for us.

And the first thing you know God is beginning to tell us there is something beyond this land. There are people beyond this land. There are joys. There are glories. There are experiences beyond this. And God doesn't make us all travelers. But we've discovered that we don't have to be. Once we've opened our mind, our consciousness, to the tremendous world about us, it begins to come to us. It comes to us in books. It comes to us in visitors. It comes to us in new experiences. It comes in interior revelations. We would never have to leave our little island and yet this whole universe could be brought right to our doorstep. And in one way or another we can enjoy the art, the literature, the sciences, the inventions, the discoveries, and the people because there always are enough of those traveling and going through and one way or another the joy would be ours of meeting them. But only if we've broken through this (head) so that we're not anchored down here to this finite sense that tells us that we're restricted to the room we're in.

Now the chick in the shell, if it could consciously think would call that its world. But then when the chick is out and it's roaming around its barnyard, it goes a step further and thinks that's its world. Well, perhaps for the chick it is but to us it isn't. We are never confined to time or space because we are not locked up in this skull. We are not even locked up in this body and this is where this 'something' that is the force that is driving us to look out to look up to look around — we're not doing it of our own accord — of our own accord we're going to stay in our shell. But something within us is nudging us, pushing us, compelling us to look around until we do become aware of this immensity all around us and of the beauty and the harmony and the joy and the companionship and the people and the past and the present and the future. And if we permit it, pretty soon we will have the feeling expressed by the Greek, "Man know thyself." And the first thing you know — the chick can't do it but we can. We can begin to think, "Who am I? Who am I? Why am I here on earth? Am I living at this moment or do I only exist from one day to the other? Is my life just an existence between the home and the office or the home and the marketplace? Is my life just an existence from one meal to the next meal, from one night's sleep to the next night's sleep? Or am I living? Am I living? Am I a part of this world? Was this world meant for me? Was I born into a corner of the world or was the whole world created and presented to me on a silver platter? Aren't the heavens mine? Isn't the earth mine?"

It was said to our ancient Hebrew prophet, "Look, look out! All of this land that you can see is yours. I give you land as far as your eyes can carry from a mountain top. The higher up you go the further you'll see. The higher you go in consciousness the wider and broader will be your vision and the more you'll see."

And the first thing you know you'll realize because it'll happen — "Why, I'm not even here. I'm not even here in this limited piece of ground. I've broken through this limitation of the skull. I'm no longer tied up inside of a skull bone. I'm not even limited to this body. All of a sudden I am I. I am I. And now as I look up and I can see 10,000 miles of sky, and 10,000 miles of ocean, and I can see people of all nations, people of all qualities, quantities — all of a sudden I find that I am I. I'm out of the shell. I'm out of the skull. I'm on a mountain top of vision and I'm hearing it."

All that you can see is yours — SEE, SEE, not with your eyesight. All that you can apprehend, all that you can comprehend, all that you can discern, anything that you can envision is yours.

The earth is the Lord's and the fullness thereof and all that I have is thine. The whole earth, the times and the tides are thine. I and my Father are one. Why, this world was created for me. I am heir to this universe — joint heir.

23. God is Only in the Still Small Voice

It is only this realization that helps you in every department of your life. This realization of the nature of Consciousness. Because Consciousness is only conscious now. And, as you look out here at these trees, you can see that they are living now. They can't live yesterday and how starved they'd be if you spoke to them about living tomorrow. In order for there to be a tomorrow for them, there has to be a continuing now. There is going to be no tomorrow for all of this foliage, and all of these trees, and all of these birds unless it is a continuing now. And so there is going to be no afterlife for anyone except as the after-life is the continuing of now.

Now watch what happens when I say to you that all that you behold out here of trees, and flowers, and birds is Consciousness expressing itself as infinite forms, and infinite varieties of forms, and infinite degrees of forms. Consciousness is appearing to you as trees, and mountains, and flowers, and birds. Consciousness is appearing to us as each other. We are only an infinite divine Consciousness manifesting itself in individual forms. The individual forms that appear as humans, animal, bird, plant life, vegetable, mineral — but Consciousness as form. The moment that you begin to perceive this can you see eternality? Because when does Consciousness stop appearing as form? No matter how fast the forms disappear, Consciousness bursts out in new forms.

We call this impersonalizing, and yet impersonalizing does not take away the love nature, it increases it. Because we can look beyond the human, animal, vegetable, that today seems to be so good and tomorrow so bad, or today so alive and tomorrow so dead, and we can love because we are loving beyond the appearance. We are loving the Consciousness that appears as infinite form.

And we are knowing that nothing can appear as form except in the nature of the Consciousness that is appearing. Therefore, we can disregard any negative appearances, finite appearances, unseemly appearances, sick or sinning or dead appearances, and only in this way can we obey the two commandments — love the Lord thy God, love thy neighbor as thyself.

You can't love all the human beings on earth — it's impossible. It's awfully difficult to love just one for a long period of time, we humans are so....whatever we are (laughter) that makes us sometimes unlovable. But we can love God supremely if we can see with the inner eye, if we can see that God — Consciousness is really appearing as form. We can love our neighbor as ourselves once we agree that Consciousness is appearing as our neighbor. Then, regardless of the finite or erroneous nature of our neighbor or other creation, we can easily realize then, that since this that we don't like is not of God, neither is it of man. If it is not in Consciousness and of Consciousness, it isn't expressed. For Consciousness can only express itself and its own qualities, and its own quantities, but it can only express itself now. And, there's the trap — we're always thinking of betterment, of improvement, of changing, but that can't be true in Consciousness, that can only be true to the finite sense with which we watch this Spiritual Consciousness evolve as form.

Inwardly, in our Spiritual vision, we become detached from these evidences of sense, and in becoming detached we have of course the secret of the Spiritual life. You remember that the One made it clear that only if you die can you experience life eternal. Only if you die and are reborn of the Spirit. Well, the only way in which you can die is to become unattached from the scene.

Let's use this example, "God is not in the whirlwind." That detaches us immediately from the whirlwind. We now have broken that sense of fear of it. God isn't in it. It hasn't any power. But temporarily we are now attached to the opposite which would be no whirlwind. So we go on from there — God is not in the whirlwind, but God is not in the opposite of the whirlwind. For God is only in the still small voice. Now we drop the whirlwind, and we drop the not whirlwind, and instantly within ourselves we realize Peace. The still small voice — the Presence of God is within us, and attachment is broken to this outer scene and by the time we look up again there is no more whirlwind. And whatever is there we are not attached to — we continue to live in the world but not of it.

24. Grace Not Dependent on Thought or Deed

Probably everybody regardless of their religious background has an idea that God's grace or God's blessing or God's giving is dependent on something. I think every religion virtually makes the receiving of God's benefits dependent on something or other. Sometimes depending on our obedience to the Ten Commandments or depending on our obedience to church rules or depending on our attendance at church or attending a communion or a religious service of some kind or fasting or sacrificing or tithing or being grateful or having faith. Yes, that's one of the tricks too — making God's grace dependent on having faith.

Well now, just as an important part of our work is releasing God in the sense of realizing that we don't need God for anything except for God to be God which God always is. In other words, we learn to stop looking to God to do something in this moment or in the future since whatever God has been doing is from everlasting to everlasting and never changes. Therefore, we understand that God could never inaugurate something now. In other words, he couldn't heal us now. He couldn't heal us tomorrow. We come to this through many steps in the Infinite Way. Firstly realizing that God is not a withholding God. Therefore, if God isn't a withholding God, God cannot be a giving God because giving now would imply withholding up to now. So therefore in God there is no such thing as giving or withholding there is only God being God. But God is being God eternally. God has been God eternally so that our function is really not to reach out to God as if we wanted something of God but rather we tune in as if we ourselves had been disconnected and we are now reconnecting ourselves with God.

Then, taking another step forward you can see that if God is responsible for the sunrise and the sunset, that these are not dependent on anything that man does or does not do. If God is responsible for the laws of nature they are operating regardless of whether man does anything to deserve it or be worthy of it or not. In other words, what God is, God is, regardless of man. And that is why at least one mystic of old had the wisdom to see that God's rain falls on the just and on the unjust. That there is no such thing as God's blessings being withheld for any reason or for any purpose or certainly, not because of anything we do or do not do.

This, of course, makes it clear that where there is an absence of God's grace it has nothing to do with God, it has to do with our violation of some spiritual law or some acceptance of a sense of separation from God but never in any wise because of God, always because of our own lack in one way or another. In other words, not even because of that lack is God withholding something.

Now, it takes a while to believe and to be able to come into the consciousness that can accept this truth that the grace of God is not dependent upon anything that man does or does not do but that man's demonstration of God's grace is dependent on his coming into conscious oneness or at-one-ment with God. Let us illustrate that. We'll take the subject of supply. Now supply is infinite and you may think that that is a metaphysical cliché but it isn't. That's an absolute truth. You need only count the blades of grass or the leaves on a tree or the amount of fruit on a tree or the amount of birds in the air or the amount of fish in the see and you will soon see that God is infinite and that supply is infinite. You need only think of the gold mines and silver mines and diamond mines and uranium mines and coal mines and begin to catch a tiny glimpse of how infinite supply is. So that there is no way at all of going to God for supply for surely God is not withholding supply.

If we individually aren't demonstrating supply, it is not because we don't go to church. It is not because we don't attend the right church. The world is still full of supply whether or not we've done these things. The answer lies in the fact that we have not known the truth. Now, when a person first learns the truth that the 121 demonstration of supply always starts with one passage of scripture we begin to understand our failure to demonstrate supply.

"What have you in the house?"

What have you in your house?

Now just think, we should have realized this ages ago, that since God is infinite and since the promise is, "Son all that I have is thine", and that God has given man dominion, it must necessarily follow that man has dominion over supply and that man has an infinity of supply. And so, the demonstration of supply is dependent not on how much we receive but how much we give out because our storehouse is already full. God is individual consciousness. God is the source of supply. Therefore, individual consciousness is the source of supply. It isn't barren. It isn't an empty storehouse. Actually, God constitutes individual consciousness.

Therefore, individual being is as infinite in substance and supply as God.

"All that I have is thine."

Now, when we accept that — "I and my Father are one" — not two. "I and my Father are one." Therefore, it is in this oneness that I have infinite supply. Now, to demonstrate that I have to start giving it, pouring it, sharing it. And I have to do it at every level of life. On the material level if I have a few drops of oil and a little meal then I have to begin sharing it — giving the first fruits to God — giving the first fruits.

But the giving and sharing of material possessions is, of course, one of the easiest of the demonstrations. But since God is spirit the major part of our demonstration is really at the spiritual level and that embraces going within ourselves and forgiving, sharing, serving, surrendering — giving up those qualities that act as a barrier to the divine. Recognizing the spiritual nature of all man kind. And in every possible way pouring it out from within ourselves. Now there hasn't been anybody in the history of the world that has learned this that has known lack or limitation because even in a circumstance like Moses with the Hebrew people where there couldn't conceivably be the supply of food or drink, he brings it forth in what seems to be miraculous ways. Or Richenbacher out in the Pacific Ocean where there certainly was no water or fresh water or food and yet they had water and they had food. So that it would be impossible to be anywhere where supply is not because it would be impossible to be any place where God is not.

Now just think that the demonstration of supply is based on one truth and that is that God or Spirit is supply. Now how much supply have we? God is the bread and the meat and wine and the water. So how much bread, meat, wine, and water do we have? God is the fortress and the high tower. How much protection and safety and security do we have?

Ah, but in our materialistic sense of life we say that a bomb proof shelter is security and we say that money is supply — thereby, cut ourselves off from the infinity of supply that is at hand and which will manifest itself in the necessary forms. The moment that we believe that supply is some of its manifested forms like coal or oil or gold or silver or diamonds or bread or meat — if we think of that as supply we've cut ourselves off from supply but it doesn't mean that there's any lack of supply. It's still infinite and it's still omnipresent.

There we go back to one of our favorite words — omnipresence. What does omnipresence mean? The omnipresence of God. The omnipresence of Spirit. The omnipresence of All-ness. The omnipresence of Life. The omnipresence of Truth, of Love, of Substance. So therefore the omnipresence of supply. Ah, but we acknowledge omnipresence in one breath and deny it in the next.

But the secret of supply is acknowledging the omnipresence. Since "I and the Father are one," in that oneness there is the omnipresence of Spirit, and Spirit is the substance of all form.

Therefore, having the substance of all form the form must appear. And our proving of that is not in looking to receive it. It is in seeking out the ways to express it. Of course, we may come to the end of our rope and believe we have nothing left but that can't be true because omnipresence is still there. The presence of God is still there. The presence of the bread of life is still there — the wine and the water. So no matter how barren we become we still are filled and it means we have to search deeper until we find what it is that we have in our house that we are keeping dammed up.

85

Now supposing we learn this lesson and supposing we begin on some particular day and say, "Well, I will set aside so and so much percentage out of everything that comes in and give the first fruits to God and share the rest with my neighbor in accordance with love thy neighbor as thyself." And we get that part of it out of the way. And then we search around and say, "Ah, yes, but what measure of un-forgiveness is locked up in me." And search around until we've got that all completed. And search around for some service that we either owe to another or even if we don't owe it, it would be loving to give it, share it. And keep on, keep on searching within our consciousness as long as there appears to be a lack. Because the only lack is in drawing it up out of our consciousness. The lack is not external to us. Now supposing we learn that lesson, we put this in to practice, and all of a sudden the abundance begins to flow. Do you not see that it never had been withheld because of God but because of our ignorance of truth? God wasn't withholding it and it didn't come to us because we did something to earn it or deserve it or be worthy of it. All we did now was come into the awareness of the truth that, "I already have it in the house."

Well, the same thing is true in healing of any situation of human experience. Whether it's a physical, mental, moral, financial, political, human relationships, whatever the healing may be. It is not because God all of a sudden deigns to do something. Nor is it because we all of a sudden have contacted God. It has to do with the fact that we have discovered the Truth and it is the Truth that sets us free.

25. The Temple of God and the Hidden Manna

In living this Infinite Way we have a principle given to us of the Master. That acts really to hold together the whole fabric of our demonstration.

"I have meat the world knows not of."

I give you this passage as one of the greatest scriptural passages ever revealed by the Master for a spiritual way of life, and one that interprets itself in human terms of success, harmony, and peace.

"I have meat the world knows not of."

Now let us see how we bring this into our lives. Everyday we become aware of some need in our experience. And so that we may turn from any fear or doubt, we instantly remember, "I have meat the world knows not of."

What is that meat?

The Master says, "I am the meat."

So it means, "I have God." — the spiritual substance of meat, wine, and water. The spiritual substance of life eternal. The spiritual substance of supply. I have it because I have God, the indwelling image of God.

"I have meat the world knows not of."

I have within me the Spirit of God which is all the meat, wine, and water I shall ever need because it will appear externally as that which satisfies every need of the moment even as the manna which was spiritual substance in the consciousness of Moses outwardly fed his followers. Just as this meat that the world knows not of, this God in the consciousness of God was the substance of the loaves and fishes that fed the multitudes and still left twelve basketfuls left over.

If you are physically, mentally, morally, or financially ill, accept this gift of God — the meat, the hidden manna, and secretly and sacredly to yourself remember, "Thank you Father, I have meat the world knows not of. I have a hidden companionship. I have a hidden source of supply. I have a hidden source of wisdom, of judgment. I have a hidden source of ideas."

Regardless of what it is that I may ever need in the external world, I have hidden within me the substance of its form — home, family, supply, companionship, joy, peace, health, freedom, safety, security — I have the substance of these, the essence of which they are formed in my understanding of this:

"I have meat the world knows not of."

I can relax from fears. I can relax from doubts. I can relax from anxiety by abiding in this word, "Thank you Father, I have meat the world knows not of."

As I abide in this — remember this is one of the pearls of great price that must not be exposed to the unprepared thought, which must not be thrown before swine to be trampled upon — this is one of the Master's gems and jewels, pearls. This is a secret that he imparted to his disciples.

"I have meat the world knows not of."

I can never hunger and thirst. And he said to you, "You will never hunger and thirst." Remember, you will never hunger and thirst because you have this hidden meat, this hidden manna, this hidden substance of all form. If you will accept the meat that I give you, if you will accept the water that I give you, you will never hunger and you will never thirst. And the meat that I give you is this hidden meat. The meat the world knows not of.

Accept it and declare to yourself, "Thank you Father, I consciously know now that I have the meat, the wine, and the water that the world knows nothing of. I have the hidden manna, the substance of all form. Except my home or my supply or my business is fed by this hidden meat it cannot endure. Except the Lord build not the house, except the Lord feed not the house, it cannot endure."

Do you see why?

It isn't outside union of peoples, of governments, of contracts in which we find strength. There has never been a law enacted that couldn't be legally broken. There has never been a contract that couldn't be broken. There has never been an agreement between nations that hasn't been broken. There has never been a human relationship, even that of parent and child that hasn't been broken, but when the Lord builds the house they labor in vain that try to destroy it. What God has brought together, no man can put asunder.

The meat that I give you, the wine and the water that I give you, no man can take from you because you see it's invisible. It is within you. It is Truth.

No one can take Truth from you, and Truth is that which I am.

Therefore, Truth is the bread, the meat, the wine, and the water. And as long as you have this Truth, as long as you accept this meat that I offer you, and wine and water, you will never hunger, you will never thirst, you will never lack, you will never fail. There is no such thing as failure in the kingdom of God. There is no such thing as failure in a life that is built on my Word.

The armies of the aliens, outnumbered the army of the Hebrews, but their Master said, "Fear not, they have only the arm of flesh, we have this hidden meat. This is our strength, not weapons. Our strength is in the hidden meat, and in the wine and the water. And this they can't reach. Their eyes cannot penetrate to the invisible. Therefore our weapons can never be touched, destroyed, harmed, nor the temple which I am."

And they rested in his Word. They rested in this Word. They rested in the assurance, "They have only the arm of flesh, but we have spiritual manna, spiritual strength, spiritual numbers — infinity." And then the enemy fought against themselves and destroyed each other so that the Hebrews did not even have to fight.

So do you find regardless of who you may believe your enemies to be or what they may be, do not depend on visible strength. Do not depend on your muscles or your arms, and even though your nation builds storehouses of arms, let your reliance be not on those arms but on the meat that I give you, on the strength that I give you, on the inspiration that I give you. I can give you meat, wine and water and if you will accept these you will never hunger or thirst. You will never want. You will never know unhappiness or failure. But you must accept the meat, wine, and water that I give you, not that the world gives you. And I give you hidden manna. I give you the Word of God which is, "I have meat — now you are accepting this Word that I am giving you, and if you accept it you can then say, 'Thank you Father, you have offered me yourself. You have offered me the hidden manna of yourself, of your kingdom within me. You have offered me infinite, eternal meat, wine, and water, and I accept.' And from this moment on I will live secretly, silently, sacredly, in the assurance that you have given and I have accepted that meat which is God. That meat which is spirit. That meat which is the spiritual substance of all form. And I accept that as an invisible substance that man whose breath is in his nostrils cannot see, cannot fight, and cannot reach."

It is therefore said in the Bhagavad-Gita that, "This life of mine cannot be burned with fire, it cannot be drowned with water, it cannot be destroyed with a knife." Why? This life of mine is invisible, incorporeal. The temple which I am is invisible, incorporeal — it cannot be drowned with water, it cannot be burned with fire, it cannot be destroyed by bullets, nor can my substance be taken from me, my supply, my home, my family, for this is the meat the Father has given me. This is the divine union of I and my Father. And in this union all that the Father hath is mine. In this union the Father says, "Son, thou art ever with me and all that I have is thine."

What does the Father have? Meat, wine, and water — life, life everlasting, life eternal. I am come — this meat the Master gave us — I am come that ye might have life, that ye might have it more abundantly. What sustains this life? The meat that I have given you. If you accept the meat, the wine, and the water, you will never hunger again, you will never thirst again. But remember your values now are changed. You are not counting the dollars in your bank. You are not counting the investments in your vaults or your properties. You're not measuring by how many bombs the government lays up. You have made a transition in this moment to the spiritual life in which I am the temple of God. I am invisible, I am spiritual, I am incorporeal, I am the temple of God in which God dwells and I have within me that meat, that wine, that water which is spiritual and which is the substance of my external safety, security, abundance, eternality.

I have within me the substance of all form — the hidden manna. I am the temple of God and I have within me hidden manna. That hidden manna is the spiritual substance, the meat, the wine, and the water of everything necessary to the harmonious, joyous, abundant life. I am the temple of God. God is in his holy temple and I have within this temple that I am, my hidden manna.

Now you know why our relationship with each other and our relationship with every Infinite Way student around the world is of a sacred nature because we are united together only by the spiritual bond of understanding, by the understanding of our relationship to God and thereby our relationship to each other. We are united in the spiritual understanding of the nature of God and the hidden manna.

Each student stands on the strength of his own conscious union with God — the source within himself. No longer is there a faith in some thought, some truth, some printed word, nor is there even salvation in obedience to a set of rules, not even the Ten Commandments. Here in the Infinite Way, faith is removed from faith in oneself — even in faith in one's own goodness — even in faith in one's own deserving or worthiness. Faith is removed from any union of any human nature and is changed in this way, "Turn ye now and live." Turn from any faith in combinations of people, change — turn ye from faith in any book of rules — turn ye from any hope — from any known source, and realize first, "The kingdom of God is within me." Deep within my own consciousness is the temple of God.

Ah, here we have it — church, temple, synagogue — these are no longer words referring to external edifices. Church, synagogue, temple. These now refer to my consciousness — your consciousness — individual consciousness. Your consciousness is the temple of God. This can be better stated since you are actually consciousness — you are the temple of God.

Ah, now we are back to the Master's teaching. "Know ye not, that you are the temple of God."

Now just think, I — and you, of course, are following me in this — I am the temple of God. God is in his holy temple. That is, God is within me. I am the temple of God. My consciousness is the temple of God. My mind is the temple of God. Know ye not that your body is the temple of God. God is the Spirit that animates your body. God breathes the life of God into you as your life so that your very life is the temple of God. YOUR life is the temple of God. Your soul is the temple of God. Your being, my being, is the temple of God. My body — God animates — Spirit animates my body.

I am the life. I am life eternal. I am the blood and the bones. The Spirit of God animates my being and body from head to foot. I am united to the entire source and creative being of life — God, by my oneness with God, by my consciousness of my oneness with God.

Now mark this. This is the most important words I have spoken today. While it is true that I and my Father are one and that I am the temple of God and even my body is the temple of God — remember that this is of no value, no benefit in my life, except through my conscious knowing it.

"Ye shall know the truth and the truth shall make you free." Not the truth shall make you free. No. The truth is the truth whether you know it or not. But if you do not know it you may be one of the thousand who fall at the left or ten thousand who fall at the right. But none of the evils of this world will come nigh the dwelling place of those who know the truth — consciously know the truth.

Therefore, I turn now from my ignorance of God and man, being and body. I turn and know the truth. Consciously now I know that I and my Father are one. Here where I am God is, for I am the temple of God. I am the holy mountain for the kingdom of God is within me. As the temple of God, God fills me — soul, being, and body, and I consciously know this truth. This is my union with God. My knowing the truth constitutes my conscious union with God. I am now consciously uniting myself with God. I have been one with God since before Abraham was but it has done me no good until this moment when I consciously open myself to the inflow and experience of God.

The kingdom of God is neither lo here or lo there. The kingdom of God is within me. You are following this because I am speaking of you. The kingdom of God is within me. I am the temple of God. And my body is the temple of God. And my home is the temple of God. And my business is the temple of God because God has built me. God has built my body. No human being knows how to build a body. God builds the temple of this body. God has built my home. "Except the Lord build the house, they labor in vain that build it." Therefore my home is built by God. My home is the temple of God, and God fills my home, every nook and cranny of it. Therefore, nothing can enter my home that defileth or maketh a lie.

God has made my marriage. Therefore, my marriage is the temple of God and that which God has united no man can break asunder. My marriage is the temple of God. My family is the temple of God. My business is the temple of God. God built my business. And God is in the temple of my business. God is the bread, the meat, the wine and the water of my business. My business is erected to God and dedicated to God — to good, to service, to quality — to the benefit of mankind, and it makes no difference if my business is a grocery business, a church business, a plantation business — when its purpose is to serve mankind it is the business of God. And God is in that business. Nothing shall enter my business that defileth or maketh a lie. If only we could know this is the truth about the steam ship business, this is the truth about the banking business, this is the truth about all business that is erected and dedicated to the service, to the benefit of mankind. Because in serving mankind we are serving God. In as much as you are serving the least of these my brethren ye are serving God. You are serving me.

What has happened to our governments, to our churches, to our homes, to our marriages, to our families, to our business, except we have left God out. We have forgotten that, "Except the Lord build the house, they labor in vain that build it."

And now in order that the lost years of the locust may be restored — in order that we may resurrect our bodies, our homes, our marriages, our business, we must turn now and live, because God has no pleasure in your failure. God has no pleasure in the failure of your business, or of your marriage, or of your home anymore than God has any pleasure in the failure of your body to show forth the glory of God.

Your body was meant to show forth the glory of God just as you and I are meant.

Why were we created? We were created in the image and likeness of God to show forth God's glory, God's bounty, God's grace.

"My peace give I unto you."

Of course, God has given us His peace. Therefore, to enjoy it we must know this. God has given me the life I am living and it is God's life that I am living because God could only give me His life. God has given me His peace so that I may have peace. God has built this temple of my body in which He may dwell — His life dwell. Therefore, my body must be a fitting temple for the holy ghost, for the Spirit of God. God has built this entire universe to show forth His glory. God has built business, industry, art, literature, religion — that God's glory may be shown forth, but until we accept, consciously accept God in the midst of us it is as if there were no God. As long as we are relying on our human relationships for our good we are not permitting God to build our lives and to function our lives.

Just as we in this room, meet together, pray together, meditate together, receive God's grace together, and unite in a most wonderful friendship, so do we understand that this is the limit of the relationship because our real life is lived in the consciousness of God's presence. Our hope, faith and dependence is not upon each other but upon the Spirit of God that in dwells me — you. God is no respecter of persons. Let it be clear that we are created equal in the sight of God regardless of race, religion, color. We are created equal in the sight of God but we only maintain that equality by maintaining the consciousness of God's presence within us. God has not removed Himself from the sinner, the sinner has removed himself from God. And the way is always open for a return. In that one single moment of turning, though your sins were scarlet you are now white as snow. Though you have kept God separate and apart from your life or your body or your business or your family — in the moment that you turn as the Prodigal turned even in his deepest extremity — in the moment that he turned he was on the way back to the father's house and the father was coming out to meet him.

In any moment, THIS MOMENT, of my turning, and recognizing God built the temple of my being that I am, God built the temple of my body, of my home, my family, my business, my marriage — in that moment I am again accepting God as the very cement that holds together the edifice of my life. God is the very cement holding together the entire edifice of every department of my life, but I consciously must bring God into every avenue of my experience so that I make of myself what I originally am — the temple of God.

26. Ten Second Meditations

The seed of Truth is not being planted, cultivated, and developed within you and me, or we would be flourishing. And to whatever extent we are not flourishing it is not the fault of God, it is the fault of our not planting, cultivating this seed of Truth within ourselves. Take this seed of Truth that I'm giving you in the same spirit as the Master offered it to us:

I can give you water, which if you drink you'll never thirst again. I can give you food, meat, which if you eat you'll never hunger again. And I say to you, I can give you a seed of Truth which if you plant within your consciousness this moment, and then cultivate it, don't plant it and go away and neglect it. Cultivate it. Day by day know this Truth—the kingdom of God is established within me, that I live and move and have my being in God. I am living not only surrounded by air but surrounded by the life and the love and the wisdom of God. I'm swimming in an ocean of God. I'm soaring and flying like the birds in the atmosphere of God. Consciously I have God dwelling in me, and I can do all things thru God that dwelleth in me, and I in Him for we are One.

God is invisible, but God is an invisible presence of intelligence and love. And this infinite invisible presence of wisdom and love is within me and without me. I am in it and it is in me. Where I am it is. Where it is I am. For we are inseparable, we are indivisible, we are One. I and my Father are One.

This is a form of contemplative meditation. Whether I orally speak it, or whether I sit here in silence with my eyes closed and think it, it is still a form of contemplative meditation. And it constitutes the activity of cultivating the seed of truth which I have planted within myself. Now, in our particular work, after our students have been with us a year or two, they set aside not less than three or four periods each day...periods of five or ten or fifteen minutes... for this particular purpose of consciously dwelling in God and consciously letting God dwell in me. And then the rest of the day we live our lives, tend to our business, art, profession, whatever it may be, the same as everyone else. The only difference between us now and the rest of the world is that we now have the Spirit of God dwelling in us because we have consciously brought it about. Now it makes no difference how many saviors there are. It makes no difference how many spiritually illumined people there are. They can bring you a temporary good, a temporary healing, a temporary supply. But it is you yourself who live with yourself 24 hours a day. And the way in which you live with yourself determines the nature of your life.

Therefore, in addition to these longer periods of meditation, we have a way of life that enables us in the midst of our normal days living to assure ourselves of the fact that we are continuing in God's Grace and under God's Grace, and that is this — we call this a ten second meditation. For this you do not have to close your eyes. You do not have to sit down. You can do it while you're driving your car. You can do it while you're in your office working. You can do it home cooking, house cleaning. Regardless of what you're doing with your body you can give ten seconds to this:

I in God and God in me. Where I am God is.

And that's enough. An hour from now:

I live and move and have my being in God. I'm swimming in an ocean of God, and God in me.

And that's enough. And another hour:

Underneath are the everlasting arms. Here where I am, God is.

And that's enough. Another hour:

I live not by might nor by power but by God's Grace. I can rest in the assurance of God's Grace.

Another hour, perhaps we can look at a tree. And realize that day or night the life of God is animating that tree and even if at this moment it seems barren, the very activity of God is the insurance or assurance that in its due season there will be fruit. And so if at the moment I appear to be barren of health or wealth or opportunity, I can realize that the presence of God in me is the assurance that in due season, I too will bear fruit richly.

So it is that never less than once in every hour there must be this ten seconds of conscious remembrance — I in God and God in me. Life by Grace — not by might or by power. Put up thy sword. Stop fighting this world. Stop fighting yourself. Stop fighting God. Put up thy sword. Be still. Be still and know that I in the midst of thee am God. Just these ten seconds now and ten seconds then is enough to keep us consciously in the atmosphere of God, and to keep ourselves surrounded with the atmosphere of God.

27. Continuing Infinite Way Healing Principles

Now let us see this clearly, what we mean by the two universes. The universe of appearance which is never God appearing no matter how good it looks, and the universe of God appearing which is the invisible kingdom. Now the Master reveals these two universes in his statement, "My kingdom is not of this world." This world is always the world of appearances — the world of sense — the world that you can see, hear, taste, touch, and smell. This is never God's universe, and if you can see it, hear it, taste it, touch it, or smell it you are not beholding God's universe. You are beholding this world. And this world can sometimes be a very good one, but it isn't the spiritual one. The spiritual one is the one that you apprehend, comprehend, discern with your inner eye when you are really seeing the man and woman of God's creating, and that's when you are seeing through them to their soul. This will explain to you then why it is that God knows nothing of sin or disease or death. These never enter the God consciousness. And the proof of this is that it never enters the consciousness of those who are God endowed. Therefore, and of course, we have only occasion to bear witness to those who are God endowed in some measure since there are so few who are fully God endowed. But remember this that the only thing that constitutes a spiritual healer or practitioner is one who is sufficiently God endowed so that sin, disease, death, or lack does not enter their consciousness even if there are 100 appearances of it out here. Only in proportion as, and in some proportion, as they can look at the crippled man and say, "What did hinder you?" In other words that crippled estate never entered the Master's consciousness. Or, look at the woman taken in adultery and say, "Neither do I condemn thee." None of the appearances enters his consciousness. All he sees whether it's in the woman taken in adultery, or the thief on the cross, or the crippled man, or the dead ones that he raised, all he sees is the spiritual reality and the appearances do not register in his consciousness. Now don't think for a moment that he didn't see them with his eyes. He saw them with his eyes just as we see with our eyes. But he had gotten to the point of spiritual endowment to where he did not react to it because he did not label them evil. He did not label them evil and therefore the healing could take place.

The moment that you can look at this appearance world and when it looks evil realize it isn't evil and when it looks good realize it isn't good, then you are at the start of a healing career. But not until you can see that conditions in and of themselves are not evil. They only have the evil that the human mind imbues them with. And it isn't your human mind or the sick one's human mind, it is the collective human mind that is being reflected by the individual.

28. The Nature of Truth

Spiritually we are equally heirs of God, children of God — heirs, joint heirs. Humanly God doesn't even know us. We aren't even known to God humanly. If God knew humans all humans would be perfect. If God knew humans every human would be healthy, wealthy, and wise. If God knew humans no human would ever die.

God doesn't know humans — not any humans because all humans have gone the way of flesh. To be known of God we must be children of God, heirs of God and to be children of God or heirs of God necessitates our doing something. Since, having accepted this dual creation, this belief of good and evil, this selfhood apart from God, this mental image of ourselves which is not ourselves — having, however, accepted this now we must do something, be reinstated in the kingdom of God.

We have been told what we must do and what we must not do. It has been pointed out to us that we must not seek an eye for an eye, a tooth for a tooth. We must not return evil for evil. A great many other things you'll find we must not do but primarily he pointed out what we must do. Love thy neighbor as thyself. Ah, of course, everybody under the canopy of heaven knows the statement, "Love thy neighbor as thyself." It has become a world cliché. Speak to most people honestly, man to man or woman to woman and you'll find that they'll say, "Yes, but it isn't practical. It was all right for them, but not for us." They couldn't be further from the truth. They haven't experimented to find out how very practical it is. Not only practical but to be honest it's the only way in which we can be reestablished in the kingdom of God.

The Sermon on the Mount must become to us a set of living principles. It must become the pattern of our existence if we are to work our way back from mortality to immortality. From being that man of earth, the natural man, to once more being that man who has his being in God. There are certain things that must be done.

We must not take thought for our life. That wipes out about all the praying for ourselves doesn't it? Take no thought for your life. Try to work that out in practical application and you'll find out how mad you can get at both God and me. God for saying it first and me for reminding you of it. Try to see how difficult it is to stop praying for yourself, for your life, for what you shall eat or what you shall drink, or where-with-all you shall be clothed, or what transportation you shall have or what home you shall have, or what companionship you shall have. Think of wiping all of those things from your thought in order that you may be children of God. In order that you might seek the realm of God, the kingdom of God — my kingdom which is not of this world. You cannot apply my kingdom, my grace, my power, my peace to this world.

Therefore, we must be healed of this world as the Master was. "I have overcome this world." I haven't improved it. I haven't enriched it. I haven't made it free. I haven't rid it of war. I have overcome it. I have wiped out of consciousness both the good and the evil. The evil and the good. Why? Because in seeking the kingdom of God, I am not seeking the kingdom of good humanness.

I am not seeking the realm of better human experience. In seeking the kingdom of God, I am seeking the kingdom of God. What is the kingdom of God? You do not know. And you never will know until you get there.

If you haven't seen Victoria Falls in South Africa you don't know what it's like. And you may have seen lots of pictures of it and lots of movies of it, but if you haven't been there you do not know what it is like. And you never will until you get there because it is beyond your expectation, it is beyond your imagination, it is beyond anything that you could possibly embrace in your thought until you see it and then there it is, now you have experienced it.

And so it is, it is folly to say, "What am I going to find when I get to the kingdom of God?" If you could be shown pictures of it, it would not tell you what it's like. If you could meet a dozen people who've been there they couldn't tell you what it's like because it is an experience and it is an experience which touches each one at their own level of consciousness. Therefore, it cannot be described.

The question is, "Why should we seek it?" And indeed it's a good question. And as long as that question is in our thought we shouldn't seek it. We wouldn't find it anyhow. So we might as well save ourselves the effort. The only reason for seeking the kingdom of God is when the first glimpse of the kingdom of God has touched our consciousness and we have a taste of it, and then we say, "Ah, ha! That's what I'm after and I will not rest until I attain it. Even if in attaining it I lose my mother and father and sister and brother. If I have to sell all that I have and give it to the poor, I will not rest." But who could make such a declaration except one who has at least had a foretaste — a glimpse — and knows that life can never be worthwhile until the kingdom of God has been attained.

And that is why many of the really great masters of the world have done a great deal to discourage people from seeking it, because it isn't to be found in spare time. Few there be that enter.

It involves a life of dedication. And there we again come up against the practical ones. "I don't have that much time." "I'm not free enough." As long as those excuses are in the thought it is better to follow them. It is folly to try to succeed while making excuses. If there is anything present in your thought greater than the attainment of the kingdom of God, the kingdom of God will not be attained. It is the pearl of great price. It is that for which you exchange everything — all of your time, all of your energy, all of your effort. And yet no one has ever been called upon to neglect the duty to their family, to their nation, to their community.

Strange but it is so.

Now see, if, and my eyes are closed, I'm looking into the dark. And if I see anything there that looks good, it only looks good or desirable because it is a mental image in my own thought, and its goodness is based on my concept of good. You may look at that very same thing and find it valueless because nothing is good or bad but thinking makes it so. There is no object in your thought that is either good or bad. It is the concept of it that you entertain that makes it good or bad to you. This object in thought actually is an illusion. That is why it has been said that, "If you attain the thing that you spend your life seeking, you'll usually find it turn to dust in your hand." It only looks glamorous afar off. The other fellow's grass always looks greener. Fame unattained looks desirable. Wealth looks as if it were the solution to every problem.

It is only after you have gained them that you find that they aren't what they appear to be. They aren't as desirable as they appear to be. Why? Because none of these things contain either good or evil. Many people seriously believe that money is evil, and it isn't. It isn't evil. It isn't good. Money is something that is dead. It reflects the value that you place upon it but in and of itself it has no quality of either good or of evil.

When your eyes are closed and you can see something or someone desirable — some condition desirable remember your thinking has made it so, it isn't so of its own accord and when you attain it you may well discover that it isn't so. Now, let us change this picture because all of this picture is in the realm of this world — the world of the pairs of opposites — the world of concepts. Now let us change that and this is what you do when you come to the spiritual healing ministry. You do not have pairs of opposites. You do not have sickness that you want to turn into health. You have no brass that you wish to turn into gold. You have no sin that you wish to turn into purity. As these touch your thought you dismiss them. Not this and not that. Not that and not that. Not this and not this. What then? Spiritual reality. I do not wish to get rid of this condition or to attain that condition. I do not wish to get rid of this lack to attain that abundance. What do I seek in my prayer? To know Thee aright. To receive Thy grace. To tabernacle with Thee. To commune with the Spirit within. These things I seek.

You have asked me for help. It may be something of a physical nature, mental, moral, financial, human relationships. But since my kingdom has nothing to do with these I'm not seriously thinking about your speech or your letter. I'm merely accepting and acknowledging the fact that here is an appearance of discord, an appearance of disharmony. And so I'm turning away from that now, not to change it into an opposite. If I succeeded I would still be in the realm of concepts. I turn within for the purpose of realizing the Spiritual nature of the universe — the Spiritual nature of God's kingdom — the Spiritual nature of God's children — the Spiritual nature of God's grace or God's law. I turn within to know the truth.

Not the truth about you as a person. Not the truth about your condition. The truth about God, and the kingdom of God, and the children of God, and the law of God. My prayer is an inner contemplation. And it lasts anywhere from a minute to all night depending on how long it takes me to find my inner peace.

Once I have found my inner peace, you aren't even in my thought. I am now present with the image of God in you — your spiritual identity, your spiritual selfhood. Just as at this moment I am not aware of you as individual students with names. I am not aware of you as people with problems or even people without problems. No, no, no, as I sit here, I am bearing witness. I am really communing with your soul. Your soul has no problems. Your soul is not in any trouble. It's joyous and free. As far as I am concerned "the world" of this room is overcome. And I am in you and you are in me and we are in God, and it's a spiritual universe, and we are spiritual children of God sharing with each other. I am telling you of my experience with God's grace, and you're telling me of your joy in God. Your freedom in God. I am in the Father and the Father is in me. You are in me and I am in you and we are in the Father — not your forms, not your figures, not your knowledge, just you. The you that God created in His own image and likeness. The you who was never born and will never die. You, pure spiritual being without opposite.

In my kingdom there is no youth and there is no age. I think that is why you'll find so many youngsters with us in our work. Because to me they aren't that. To me there is no youth and there is no age. We are children of God. We are spiritual offspring of the Father. We are the Sons of God, the image of God. There's no one younger than another, no one older than another because there is no such thing as age in the kingdom of God. No pairs of opposites. No young and no old. No strong and no weak — just one pure spiritual being. I am that. Thou art that. We are that. For we are one in our spiritual identity. One in the same eternal being. One in the same immortal being. In this consciousness there's no one to be healed.

There is only the God of your identity to be realized. With spiritual discernment we can see through the shell of your appearance to that spiritual spark which is you. Know ye not? Know ye not that you are the temple of God? No one can ever say that to you while they are looking at your form. No one can ever say that to you when they're looking at your age or your bank account. No one can ever say that to you. It is only when they can see through the shell to the soul. Then they can say, "Know ye not? Ye are the temple of God. Know ye not? Your body is the temple of God." This is not the body you see in the mirror, this is the body that is invisible, incorporeal, spiritual, and eternal. The body that you have and that you had before you were born and that you will have when you leave this plane. The incorporeal, spiritual body — the gift of God.

29. Instructions for Teaching the Infinite Way - God, Prayer

Continuously I am receiving letters saying that so and so is using my books and not giving me credit, and so and so is quoting me, and my answer is "I didn't invent those things. They were a gift of God, but not to me. They were just a gift of God to spread." Why do I copyright my writings? Well, don't think I copyright them so as to have an exclusive on them, but no responsible publisher would publish them without. So they have to be copyrighted. Aside from that I would prefer that they not be copyrighted.

Earnings? I would earn more if they weren't copyrighted because the little royalties that I get would be more than made up by people's gratitude for their healing and the regeneration that they get. And as a matter of fact, my biggest source of income is the voluntary money that is sent in to me. It's far, far — many times bigger than my royalties. So if there were four times more books out, I'd have four times more earnings. Do you see that? So even from a selfish standpoint I wish they weren't copyrighted. But from a spiritual standpoint more so because any revelation that I have had, as you can see I can back it up with Buddha, and I could back it up with Nanak. See that? So that it didn't originate with me. It really just came through me. And so it isn't mine. And if they don't want to mention my name fine.

In the last analysis I explained to our students that God will be the only salvation of the world— the Spirit of God in man. No man or woman will save the world ever. But every man and woman from the original Krishna down who has ever lent themselves to a spiritual ministry is a step on the stairway.

This world cannot be saved on the teachings of any one individual because they'd be locked up in a book or they'd be locked up in somebody's memory, they have to go into somebody else to carry out. Do you see? Many of these teachings of the Bible were in the Hebrew Testament — first commandment, the second commandment of the two great commandments — they didn't originate with him. Lean not unto thine own understanding, whither shall I flee from thy spirit — omnipresence, omniscience — it's all...and you'll find it in the Oriental scriptures too if you'll just know how to look.

So it is then that all these people have been contributors. But it is the activity of the image of God, the Spirit of God in man, which ultimately will save him from his mortality. We will only put off mortality not by humanly wanting to but as this Spirit of God touches us inside and puts it away. No man can of himself be good or worthy.

In Australia I was to meet a minister after his noon broadcast — he'd been reading the books and wanted to know more. And so we listened to his noon broadcast and then met him at the radio station and we went for a long afternoon drive.

And the first thing he said was, "I suppose you could pick my remarks to pieces."

And I said, "No, no, no. I must say that I was in agreement with everything you said but one. And, evidently you have a fine ministry and are doing a great work. But there was one thing that you said that I could never come into agreement with. You told them that if they choose they could come to your church on Sunday and be on the right side as it were and so forth and so on — receive the blessings and all this and that."

And I said, "That I'll never agree with. I do not believe that they have that choice or that they could make that decision."

"Why," he said, "that's the foundation of our teaching."

I said, "Then your foundation is wobbling."

And just then there was a man coming down the street rip-roaring drunk. And he was in a horrible shape — his clothing, his face, his conduct, everything.

So I said, "Let us pull up here to the side."

Now I said, "Sir, you have a nice church and a good family and what we call success in life?"

"Yes."

"And so have I, and so I'm very happy. You're happy?"

"Yea."

"And this [drunk] man is seeking happiness and a family and prosperity?"

"Yes."

"Let's call him over and tell him come to church Sunday and get it. We've got what will give him what he's seeking."

"Oh, no," he said, "I don't think he has the choice."

Of course he hasn't got the choice. Of course he hasn't. His consciousness hasn't even got in it an awareness that we exist or that we have anything, so how could he have a choice?

Now I said, "I can go back to my own younger days when people tried to convince me of going to church or doing this, that, or the other thing, and I had no choice I just couldn't go."

30. Infinite Way Prayer

"Prayer is the word of God that comes to you when you are silent enough, still enough, and expectant to receive it." - Joel S. Goldsmith

The Omnipotence of I

This work is to be read as the Voice from within, speaking to you. It is not to be interpreted as a person speaking.

Be not afraid, I am with you. Be not afraid of those out there: I am He. I am here, and I am there. Be not afraid: I in the midst of you am mighty. I am life eternal. I am the way. Just rely on Me. Fear no danger, for there is no power external to you. I in the midst of you am infinite power, the all-power, the only power.

Live by Grace, since I am your meat, your wine, your water. I can give you water, and if you drink of it you will never thirst again. I have meat the world knows not of. I am the resurrection. I am the way: I am the way to your peace; I am the way to your abundance; I am the way to your safety.

I am the rock. I am a fortress. I am a high tower. Abide in Me and let Me abide in you, and no evil shall come nigh thy dwelling place. No weapons that are formed against thee shall prosper. Why? They are shadows; they are not realities; they are not powers. I in the midst of you am omnipotence, the only power. These arrows, these poisoned darts, these germs, these bullets, these bombs: they are shadows. They are beliefs in a power apart from Me. They are a universal belief in two powers. Believe in Me as Omnipotence.

God Alone is the Source

Of course, I haven't enough understanding and I never shall have enough understanding to heal anyone or anything. Health does not come through my understanding. This health must come as the activity of God, not because of my understanding — not because of what I know, or do not know. I am a willing instrument, Father. I am willing to be still; I am willing to let the activity of Thy being be my being and Thy grace the sufficiency unto this individual or this situation. "I can of mine own self do nothing. . . ." I, the Son, am but the instrument for I, the Father.

Your Grace is My Sufficiency

Father, I have great tasks today that are beyond my understanding and beyond my strength, and so I must rely on You to perform that which is given me to do.

You have said that You are ever with me and all that You have is mine. Grant me the assurance today that Your love is with me, that Your wisdom guides me, and that Your presence upholds me.

Your grace is my sufficiency in all things. Your grace! I am satisfied, Father, to know that Your grace is with me. That is all I ask because that grace will be made tangible as manna falling from the sky, as a cruse of oil that never runs dry, or as loaves and fishes that keep ever multiplying. Whatever my need, Your grace provides for it this day.

Since God is My Consciousness

Since God is my consciousness, and God, or Truth, fills my consciousness and is the substance and activity of it, that Truth is the substance and activity of it, that Truth is the substance of the form of everything within my universe, even if it appears as a tree or a flower, an enemy or a friend. Everything in my universe responds to that awareness.

I embrace my universe within my consciousness, a universe formed of, and by, that consciousness; and because my consciousness is filled with Truth, my universe manifests the activity, quality, and substance, the nature and the character of Truth, of eternality and immortality.

I stand at the doorway of my consciousness, permitting nothing of a discordant nature to enter, maintaining it in its purity as that place through which God flows to all the world. All who enter my spiritual household, my temple, find therein the peace and joy which become the substance of their being, their bodies, or their pocketbooks. This God-consciousness envelops them, governs and sustains them, and reveals this truth as the truth of their own individual being, so that they, in their turn, become a law not only to themselves but to all who look to them for help.

God Constitutes Individual Being

God expresses itself as individual being. Regardless of the appearance or of the degree of mortality that is presenting itself to my eyes and ears — whether it is the criminal, the insane, the dying, or the dead — regardless of all appearances, God alone is, and God alone is the entity and identity of all being.

God constitutes individual being. God is the life, the Soul, the Spirit, and the mind of individual being; God is the law unto individual being. Even the body is the temple of God.

God constitutes individual being, and therefore the nature of individual being is godly and good, and in it there is nothing that "defileth...or maketh a lie." (Revelation 21:27)

When Ye Pray

I come here for prayer and meditation in the full knowledge that I am not going to a person, although the relationship between God and me is as personal as that between father and son or mother and son, but I am turning to the Spirit of wisdom and love whose will it is that I bear fruit richly.

I am not entering the Presence of God in order to enlighten God. I am not going to God to present my views to Him, hoping to tell Him more than He already knows or to tell Him what is good for me to have. I do not expect through this period of prayer and communion to influence God in my behalf.

I turn to God that He may fill me full of Himself, fill me full of His wisdom, His peace and glory, and make me a fitting instrument on earth for His love.

My Grace is Your Sufficiency

"My grace is sufficient for thee. . . .I will never leave thee, nor forsake thee." Why struggle as if you had to hold on to Me? Why struggle as if you had to seek for Me and search for Me? I am in the very midst of thee, "closer. . .than breathing, and nearer than hands and feet."

If you know how to give good gifts to your children, how much more do I, your heavenly Father, know? Do not struggle for them. I will give them to you. I will give you water: do not lower bucket for it. Do not strive. I will give you water. You, you be still. Let Me feed you. Let Me satisfy your thirst. Let Me, at the center of your being, be the healing influence, the healing God.

Do not try to make your mind or your thoughts the healing God. "My thoughts are not your thoughts, neither are your ways my ways." Why do you not give up your thoughts and give up your ways? Let My thoughts take over. You just rest and listen to Me — the still small voice at the center of your being.

I will never leave you. I will never forsake you. Even in "the valley of the shadow of death," I will be there. You will never know death; you will never die. Why? Because I give you living waters that spring up into life everlasting.

And so if you are listening for My still voice, if you are resting in My everlasting arms, if you are relaxing in Me, if you are letting every word that proceedeth out of My mouth feed you, maintain and sustain you, you will never die.

I have never known a righteous man to beg bread. What is a righteous man? Only he who rests in his union with Me. Rest, then, in the contemplation of My love and My presence. My spirit is with you. My presence goes before you.

"In my Father's house are many mansions. . . .I go to prepare a place for you." I do. Stop thinking, then. Stop, stop, stop fearing; stop doubting. Stop trying to hang on to sentences and words and affirmations and denials. Let go; rest in My bosom; rest in My arms. I, your heavenly Father, know that you have need of these things, and it is My good pleasure to give them to you — not make you struggle and strive for them, not make you treat for them, but give them to you through grace. Not by might, not by power, but by My spirit. You can do all things through Me, the God of your being.

I Am Here as a Transparency

"My consciousness now is the temple of God. All self-interest and self-desire are absent from this temple. I am here only as a transparency for the Spirit of God; I am here only that all in the world who are seeking light may find entrance to my consciousness and be illumined. I am here for only one purpose, that the sick reaching out for wholeness, the sinner reaching out for forgiveness, the dying reaching out for life, may find entrance into this tabernacle which I am and from which all sense of self is absent, so that the benediction which is the grace of God may touch all who enter here.

I Know Not What You Are

"God, I know not what You are, or even how to pray to You. I know not how to go in or how to come out; I know not what to pray for. "I cannot believe in the God that the world has accepted, for I have seen the fruitlessness and frustration which follows such blind faith. I must find the God whom no man knoweth, the God that is, the one true God that created the universe in His own image and likeness — perfect, harmonious, and whole — and who maintains and sustains it in its infinite and eternal perfection. In such a God I can believe.

"Reveal Yourself, Father; show me Your will. Never again will I dishonor You by trying to tell You what I need and then attempt to coerce You into delivering it. Never will I expect You to do my will or my bidding — to be my messenger boy. "I place my life, my hand, my being, and my body in Your keeping. Do with them what You will, Father. Take my sins, my fears, and my diseases; take my health, and my wealth; take it all. I ask only one gift — the gift of You, Yourself."

My Kingdom is the Reality

"This world is not to be feared or hated or loved: this is the illusion, and right where the illusion is, is the kingdom of God, My kingdom.

"My kingdom is the reality. This, that my eyes see or my ears hear, this is the superimposed counterfeit, not existing as a world, but as a concept, a concept of temporal power. "My kingdom is intact; My kingdom is the kingdom of God; My kingdom is the kingdom of the children of God; and My kingdom is here and now.

"All that exists as a temporal universe is without power. I need not hate it, fear it, or condemn it: I need only understand it."

Why Am I Seeking?

"God! Why am I seeking God, when God is already closer to me than breathing? Why am I struggling so hard to reach God? Why am I going through so many mental gymnastics? Why do I think I have to repeat formulas? Why should I believe that I have to stand on my head, or fast, or feast to find the God that is already my very own being? True, judging from appearances, I am separate and apart from God, but what is the truth? What truth is there other than that I and the Father are one?

"God is; I am. I am not meditating to find God. I am meditating only to bring to conscious remembrance the truth that I and the Father are one that the place whereon I stand is holy ground. All that God is, I am, for He has said, 'Son, thou art ever with me, and all that I have is thine.'

"Here and now all that the Father has is mine: wisdom, life, love, peace, confidence, serenity, and joy. I need not struggle physically or mentally for these. I need not go any place to find them because here where I am God is — I in God, and God in me.

"This is the truth about me; this is the truth about my patient; this is the truth about my family. There is really no family but God's family since there is only one Father: 'Call no man your father upon the earth: for one is your Father, which is in heaven.' We are all of one household.

"God in the midst of me is my life, the bread on my table, the meat and the wine and the water. God 'is the health of my countenance.' "I do not have to go anywhere; I do not have to think anything.'Be still, and know that I am God.' I is God. I is infinite. I is all-inclusive. In the presence of the I, there is fulfillment.

"Where the Spirit of the I is, there is peace, joy, completeness, and harmony. I do not have to deserve it: God's rain falls alike on the just and on the unjust. I have only to be still because it is 'not by might, nor by power' that this is realized: it is 'in

quietness and in confidence.' In quietness and confidence. I know the presence of God is here with me even though I cannot feel it."

I Am God's Responsibility, Not My Own

"God sent me forth in expression, and I am God's responsibility, not my own. In that assurance, I can rest, for in that moment, in some measure, the kingdom of God comes to earth for me. "A thousand may fall at my left, and ten thousand at my right, but as long as I abide 'in the secret place of the most High,' no evil can come near my consciousness or dwelling place. Nothing can touch my inner being as long as I live, not by might or by power, not by taking thought for my life, by battling evil, or hoping God will destroy my enemies, but by God's grace. I rest in quietness and in confidence in the assurance that God is the creator, the maintainer, and sustainer of all that is."

God is the Self of Me

"God is the Self of me, and therefore, it is my Self that is omnipresent, omnipotent, omniscient. It is not some self from thousands of years ago. It is not some self that is up in heaven. It is my Self, thy Self, our Self, the one infinite, divine Self which is omnipresent, omniscient, omnipotent, the Self of me.

"If I mount up to heaven, I have this Omnipotence, Omniscience, and Omnipresence with me, but if, temporarily or in belief, I walk through hell or 'the valley of the shadow of death,' I need only say, 'I,' and smile at the idea that I could ever have accepted a limited self that was born and will die, when there is only one Self, and that is the God-Self.

"The outer self is the masquerade which is born of the belief in two powers, but I am spiritual Being.

"I am nothing that can be seen, heard, tasted, touched, or smelled. I am nothing that anyone can get his mind or his fingers on because I am nowhere between the toenails and the top of the head. No one can grasp Me because if he tries he will get his hands on nothing. I, Consciousness, Spirit, am nothing tangible, nothing physical, nothing mortal, nothing material, and in that non-tangibility or in-corporeality you have Me as I am, that I AM which I was in the beginning with God, incorporeal real Selfhood."

I am the Image of God Made Manifest!

"I am not a human being! I never was a human being! I am the image of God made manifest! God, Himself, goes forth into expression as the Son of God. None of the trials and tribulations or sins of the present, past, or future, can ever attach

110

themselves to that which I am. God, Himself, went forth as the Son into the world, to manifest the image of God, to show forth the mind that is God, to show forth the Spirit, Soul, and body of God. I am the very body of God, the temple of the living God, the temple of the Holy Ghost—the very presence of God, Itself, made manifest as individual being."

God's Function is to be God

"God is! God's function is to be God, Good. God's activity is expressing Itself as life, truth, love, as the rhythmic flow of the grace of God, just as the tides are changing at this moment, as the sun is in motion at this moment, and the stars, and in this moment as the grass is growing. Sap in the center of the trees is rising and ultimately will come forth as fruit. That is all taking place in the now. Even though in the bitter cold of winter, we might look at the tree and behold it barren, yet within, God is fulfilling Itself, and in their due season, leaves, buds, blossoms, and fruit will appear—all by the grace of God."

I am that Place in Consciousness

"Father, all Your wealth is mine; all Your life is my life; all the intelligence of You is the intelligence of me; and I am a witness to all Thou art. I am that place in consciousness through which You can manifest and express."

BN Publishing

Improving People's Life

www.bnpublishing.com

CPSIA information can be obtained at www.ICGtesting.com
Printed in the USA
LVOW112257231212

312990LV00010B/412/P